PUBLIC SECTOR INVESTMENT PLANNING FOR DEVELOPING COUNTRIES

PUBLIC SECTOR
INVESTMENT PLANNING
FOR
DEVELOPING COUNTRIES

E. V. K. FITZGERALD

Assistant Director of Development Studies
University of Cambridge

0840804

HOLMES & MEIER PUBLISHERS, INC.
IMPORT DIVISION
IUB Building
30 Irving Place, New York, N.Y. 10003

First published 1978 by
THE MACMILLAN PRESS LTD
London and Basingstoke
Associated companies in Delhi Dublin
Hong Kong Johannesburg Lagos Melbourne
New York Singapore and Tokyo

Printed in India by
THE MACMILLAN INDIA PRESS
Madras

British Library Cataloguing in Publication Data

FitzGerald, Edmund Valpy Knox
    Public sector investment planning for developing
    countries.
    1. Capital investments 2. Underdeveloped areas –
    Capital 3. Underdeveloped areas – Government
    business enterprises
    I. Title
    658.1′527   HG4028.4

    ISBN 0–333–22627–5
    ISBN 0–333–22628–3   Pbk

For Angelines

CONTENTS

II. THE PLANNING OF PUBLIC INVESTMENT

III. SUPPLEMENTARY MATERIAL

PREFACE

THIS book is the product of postgraduate teaching of and professional experience in the analysis of public investment in developing countries over a number of years. The conceptual and theoretical methodology for such analysis appears to be approaching general agreement on many points now, particularly through the combined efforts of the international aid agencies, complemented by the accumulation of detailed case studies throughout the Third World. None the less, despite the existence of several excellent theoretical manuals on project appraisal, there does seem to be a need for a practical text to bridge the gap between theory and practice. Certainly, the experience of compiling reading lists for postgraduates at Cambridge and planning officers in the field indicates that the standard bibliography lacks a practical book aimed at the needs of developing countries–a lacuna which the present volume attempts to fill in a modest way.

The presentation of the material retains many of the characteristics of the lecture course upon which it is based, particularly the illustration of analytical points by numerical example and the provision of problems to be worked out separately. The resulting style is somewhat heterogeneous, but as this has been found useful by those using the initial version,* it has been retained. Specific gratitude must first be expressed to Sandy Robertson, for collaboration in the creation of the 'workshop' exercise reproduced at the end of the book, and to Andrew Nickson of the UNDP for patiently checking the numerical examples throughout. Acknowledgement is due to the Cambridge University Examinations Syndicate for permission to quote from past examination papers. Above all, I would like to thank Iain Little and Maurice Scott for their support, the Director and staff of the Cambridge Course on Development for their unfailing help and encouragement, and the students from three continents who have made this book possible.

St Edmund's House　　　　　　　　　　　E. V. K. FITZGERALD
Cambridge
Michaelmas Term, 1976

Project Appraisal and Microplanning in the Public Sector, Course on Development, Cambridge (mimeo, September 1973).

INTRODUCTION

It is generally recognised, by governments and international agencies alike, that public investment analysis is an integral and essential part of economic planning. On the one hand, the individual investment project is the concrete manifestation of the development plan, while on the other the sum of such development projects makes up most of the state capital budget. Many experts would suggest, moreover, that a lack of practical attention to project analysis in the past has led to inadequate public investment planning and the failure of sectoral programmes, and that although considerable advances have been made recently in the theory of such analysis, this has not yet been translated into a completely practical methodology.

As far as public sector analysis is concerned, in contra-distinction to purely private investment, there are four distinct categories of state investment to be examined:

(1) public infrastructure projects such as roads and water supplies;
(2) public enterprise projects such as steel mills and power plant;
(3) public credit for private sector projects such as rural co-operatives and small industry;
(4) private sector projects subject to public control such as transport and mining ventures.

The growth of this public investment to the point where in many developing countries it provides the bulk of capital formation has tended not only to change the view of such activity from one of 'infrastructural support' to one of 'economic leadership', but also to make planners more aware of the need for a distinct methodology that reflects the economic and social aims of the state rather than those of private capital. This may be just as important in cases where the domestic entreprenuerial group is weak and thus the state is the only force capable of resisting or controlling the penetration of foreign enterprise and supporting local capital, as it is when an explicit transition to socialism is involved.

The 'social' dimension of public sector project analysis covered in this book is the appraisal of investment in such a way as to assess the economic contribution to the nation as a whole – so-called 'cost–benefit analysis' – within a broad definition of development that includes the criteria of income redistribution and autonomous industrialisation. Such an approach contains as much judgement as objective measurement, and is therefore as much an art as a science: all that a methodology can do is provide a logical basis for the formulation of these judgements and the exploration of their implications. In consequence, projects should not be considered in isolation but as part of an overall sectoral programme, and although the use of shadow prices allows a considerable degree of separation to be maintained, the importance of a project (and in many cases the valuation of its output) depends upon its place in a sectoral development programme, which is why the topic of 'microplanning' must be considered in conjunction with project appraisal proper.

In recent years there has grown among project analysts working in the field an awareness that there is a real and pressing need for 'sociological inputs' to the planning of public investment. This is to some extent the natural consequence of the addition of economic to engineering criteria over the past two decades, but has mainly been influenced by the realisation among development specialists that there is another dimension than the purely economic – the objective of aggregate output growth must be redefined to include considerations such as distribution and ownership. This concern has recently been made more specific by attempts to organise 'poverty focused aid' and thus the operational need to introduce explicit distributive criteria: methods of handling this are discussed in this book. At another level, rapidly accumulating experience of practical difficulties in project implementation has resulted in project planners and aid organisations stressing the need for greater prevision of administrative problems and participant response. To some extent these problems are already implicitly included in the estimates made by, say, an agronomist of the anticipated increase in crop yields consequent upon irrigation, or by engineers of the period needed for constructing a bridge, but there is clearly a need for their more explicit treatment in project reports – in spite of (or perhaps because of) the embarrassment that may be involved.

However, this latter response is largely an 'instrumentalist' one in that it is concerned with 'making the project work', which is not the same as an approach geared to the inclusion of social criteria in planning as such would be. In other words, the current view seems to be that social factors should be included as constraints rather than as part of the objective function itself. None the less, quite fundamental social problems can be expressed in a specific way, and interpreted in terms of alternative project designs without reducing the rigour or objectivity of the analysis.* Moreover, although any attempt at planning society will necessarily result in the imposition of a certain pattern of change from outside the particular community concerned, and thus the subordination of the internal dynamic to some wider strategy and broader vision of the future, this will be also true of all forms of economic development in the real world. Above all, that form of development brought about by 'market forces' (i.e. capitalist competition) will impose violent change on traditional communities. The only possibility is that their interests should be taken into account; they cannot be granted sufficient power for autonomous development and also remain isolated from the economy as a whole.

This is not, however, the main reason for largely omitting social or environmental considerations from this book, and nor is the conventional author's stratagem of claiming lack of space. The problem with social aspects of project planning, in the present state of our knowledge at least, is that the relevant considerations tend not to be generalisable in the form of widely applicable criteria in the way that microeconomic analysis can be. Field experience can all too easily be reduced to anecdote, and sociological theory only leads to broad statements of no very immediate applicability: at present this branch of the social sciences appears to have to the descriptive power of economics, but not its prescriptive capacity.

The methodology presented in this book is inevitably based upon the assumption that the government concerned 'takes planning seriously'. In other words, a situation obtains where the state exercises sufficient control over the processes of production and accumulation to enable it to use planning as a means of achieving specific development objectives rather than merely as a way of raising foreign loans. In consequence, this implies that the application of the methodology in many economies characterised not only by a state subordinate to a dependent capitalist structure but also by a disarticulated public sector can be highly misleading. Even in the case of a recognisably 'developmentalist' state, the degree to which particular aspects such as income distribution criteria can be applied will depend upon the class support for the government rather than the aims of the planners them-

---

*See the 'Alpha–Beta Fisheries Project' in Part III, p. 165 below.

selves. This caveat is not intended as an admonition or even as a severe limitation on applicability but rather as a reminder to the reader to distinguish the normative from the positive in economics.

Experience of teaching the subject of this book to postgraduates both at Cambridge and overseas had demonstrated that the major difficulties encountered by the student are not to be found in the internal logic of project appraisal and microplanning, which is, after all, quite simple. Rather the problems that tend to emerge are three: inexperience in applying the standard techniques to a practical situation; lack of appreciation of the relationship of the subject matter to the wider themes of development planning; and the propensity to seek for a single 'correct' methodology. Within the limited scope of such a small volume, it is hoped to meet these three difficulties in a similar fashion as has been done in the classroom. Facility in the application of technique in best acquired, naturally enough, by supervised experience in the field, but in default of this (or prior to it) short fictional examples have been found to be more useful than elaborate case studies, because those latter cannot hope to provide the necessary background material except in an absurdly synthetic manner, and do not often illustrate an analytical point clearly. The link between the methodology and wider development issues is often overlooked in courses dedicated exclusively to 'project appraisal', although in reality many aspects of this cannot be resolved without reference to those issues, and indeed such a discussion often permits them to be brought down to a practical plane. To take but two examples: the estimation of the shadow wage rate requires a specification and quantification of the effects of agricultural productivity, internal migration and the pattern of accumulation in the economy; and the application of the input–output matrix to sectoral production programming requires that the concept of intersectoral integration be defined in an operational form. Finally, the familiar quest (and request) for a single methodology (or better, textbook) often reflects a somewhat naive view of microeconomics itself – as if it were a branch of mechanical engineering – so that a running critique of the techniques taught, in terms of both their theoretical assumptions and their strategic implications, is clearly necessary at all stages.

This book is organised in three parts. The first covers the analysis of public sector projects, and is concerned with the exposition of financial and economic investment criteria, the evaluation of resource and factor inputs to a project and the introduction of income distribution objectives to the methodology, concluding with a discussion of some of the recent 'problems and advances' in cost–benefit analysis. The second part is concerned with the topic of 'micro-planning', and covers the relationship between plans and projects, the programming of investment in time and space, capital budgeting and some of the recent developments in the subject. The third part consists of an assortment of material that may be of use to the reader – a 'workshop exercise', a selection of questions from recent Cambridge examinations, a set of discount tables, and finally a bibliography. As was mentioned in the Preface, this makes for a somewhat heterogeneous presentation – but the objective is utility to the student and planner rather than academic elegance. At the end of each chapter reference is made to appropriate additional reading, so that particular topics can be pursued further.

THE PATTERN OF CAPITAL ACCUMULATION IN SOME DEVELOPING COUNTRIES

(Per cent of Gross Fixed Capital Formation in the early nineteen seventies)

	General Government	Other Public Sector*	Total Public Sector	Private Sector	Total GFCF
Bangladesh	..	..	87	13	100
Brazil	22	30	52	48	100
India	21	22	43	57	100
Kenya	22	16	38	62	100
Mexico	20	28	48	52	100
Nigeria	..	..	42	58	100
Peru	21	22	43	57	100
Tanzania	23	21	44	56	100

*Including state enterprises, decentralised authorities, etc.
Sources: Brazil, Mexico, Peru – UN/ECLA Economic Survey; India – National Accounts Statistics; Kenya – Statistical Abstract; Nigeria – Third National Development Plan; Bangladesh – First Five-Year Plan; Tanzania – Economic and Statistical Review; IMF International Financial Statistics.

PART I

THE ANALYSIS OF PUBLIC SECTOR INVESTMENT PROJECTS

CHAPTER 1

PROJECT APPRAISAL

PROJECT appraisal as a planning technique has grown rapidly in popularity and application over the past decade, and has almost come to form a method of development planning on its own. The object of this part of the book is to explain the main elements of what has by now become an almost 'standard' approach to public investment analysis in developing countries, with criticism where appropriate, while paying particular attention to those aspects that indicate the connexion with the planning process as a whole on the one hand and with the role of the state within the economy on the other.

To this end, this part has been organised as follows. After a brief history of the subject and some comments on project presentation, which make up the rest of this chapter, we explore the investment criterion in some detail. This is followed by an analysis of the principles of economic resource valuation, the treatment of the factors of production and the quantification of external costs and benefits. Finally, the contentious topic of 'distributional weighting' is taken up, before some concluding remarks on project appraisal as a whole and a set of examples to be worked through.

A Brief History of Project Appraisal

Although cost–benefit analysis as a technique of economic evaluation for public investment can be traced back to the middle of the nineteenth century, its active life really starts in the 1930s when, with the American 'New Deal' public works programme, the U.S. Corps of Engineers devised a methodology to justify

1

dam projects to the Congress. The method was crude, being based on the expected increase in farmers' net income and the profits on electricity generated, but it contained the essential elements of the present approach.* The accounting methods for appraising *private* investment dates, of course, from the book-keeping of Renaissance merchants, but again, cash-flow analysis is a comparatively recent technique, only gaining acceptance in the business community since the Second World War.

Project appraisal, however, in the sense that it is discussed in this book, is a method scarcely a quarter of a century old. As a planning technique in developing countries, it was first applied by international agencies such as the United Nations and the World Bank. The first recognisable 'manual' was produced by the UN Commission for Latin America in 1958 (UN, 1958), but this was mainly concerned with forecasting method, there being little discussion of externalities and shadow pricing, while the investment criterion itself was not clearly defined. Throughout the 1960s a lively debate among development planners both academic and practising took place over the proper criteria to be used. In particular, much of this debate centred on the opportunity cost of labour and the effect of the choice of technique (i.e. capital-intensity) on accumulation over time – the important early papers on this being Lewis (1954) and Galenson and Leibenstein (1955), respectively. By the middle of the decade a consensus was beginning to emerge on the outlines of project appraisal technique, based upon the principles of 'discounted flows' and the application of the theory of comparative advantage, which would allow projects to be analysed separately from the rest of the economic planning process. This seemed at the time to get round the difficulties encountered with the introduction of 'national planning' to a large number of mixed economies, which had led to considerable disillusionment, and thus was accepted with considerable enthusiasm by the 'aid' agencies. This methodology is best set out in OECD (1968) and UNIDO (1972), and has also been adopted by bodies such as the World Bank, the Ministry of Overseas Development in Britain and various Regional

---

*See Prest and Turvey (1965), the earliest reference being J. Dupuit, 'Sur la Mesure d'Utilité des Travaux Publiques', *Annales des Ponts et Chaussées* (Paris, 1844).

Development Banks. Meanwhile the somewhat different methods used in the developed economies, especially the United States and the United Kingdom, were evolving to cover external effects from public infrastructure projects, particularly transport, thereby influencing methodology for use in poorer countries.

Despite this emergence of a new 'orthodoxy', there remain areas of considerable disagreement, perhaps the most important being the connexion between project appraisal and the rest of the planning process. The international agencies, as might be expected, have tended to minimise this problem, probably out of a desire not to get involved with broader issues and retain control over 'their' projects. The developing countries themselves, if such generalisation is possible, recovering from the disillusion of national planning at the end of the decade, have been strengthening the project divisions of their planning ministries and in the process discovering that in practice project appraisal must be integrated into the sectoral planning and capital budgeting systems.

The subject is, then, a comparatively new one by the standards of the history of economic theory, but one which has managed to establish the basis for an agreed orthodoxy, leaving a considerable but well-defined area for debate. As far as application is concerned, however, there is a great deal of ground to be made up, both in the training of planning officers and in the establishment of the appropriate administrative procedures.

The Presentation of a Project Analysis

The preparation of a project report is a complex task, the nature of which can only be sketched here. It should naturally form a part of the overall planning process (see Part II) and be the result of a 'pre-feasibility study' carried out by the appropriate government body, this having already determined in broad terms the objectives and the alternative means (sizes, locations, designs, etc.) to be examined – these being stated in the 'Terms of Reference' (see below). The Project Report is also commonly called a 'Feasibility Study', and should be the main basis for an executive decision on acceptance, modification or rejection.

The team preparing a project report will generally be multi-disciplinary, made up of engineers (civil, industrial, agronomic, etc.) and economists specialised in investment analysis and the sector in question. In recent years there has been a tendency not only for the economists to 'lead' the team, but also towards the inclusion of sociologists and experts on the natural environment. In the past most major studies have been carried out by consultants, usually foreign in the case of international finance, but recently there has been a shift towards the use of government teams, calling on specialist advice as required.

Although the presentation of project reports can differ considerably, there are six main components, the contents of which are broadly as follows:

(1) *Terms of Reference*: the definition of the objectives of the study, outline of project alternatives, topics to be covered, etc. This provides a guideline for the project team, and is based on the pre-feasibility study.

(2) *Engineering Study*: the physical characteristics of the project, the design of constructions and plant, the technical aspects of 'output' (e.g. crop production, power supply), timetable for execution and so on. This establishes whether the project is technically feasible.

(3) *Financial Study*: estimates of the direct costs of construction and plan at market prices, using 'quantity survey' techniques, possibly studies of the market, and financial appraisal on an accounting basis. This establishes how much the project will cost in budgetary terms.

(4) *Cost–benefit Analysis*: appraisal of the economic costs and benefits of the project and alternatives, its impact on the economy and on the incomes of those affected. This establishes whether the project should be accepted or not.

(5) *Implementation*: this is mainly concerned with the administrative requirements of the project (e.g. responsibilities of government departments), but also should contain examination of the social and environmental implications of the project.

(6) *Conclusions and Recommendations*: a short summary of the report as a whole, suitable for presentation at the highest executive level.

This report, when complete, goes to the relevant ministerial department, to the planning authority and possibly also to the financing agency. If it is accepted, then the final design stage can be started, followed by the construction and the entry into operation.

This last task, although clearly of crucial importance if full use is to be made of the investment, has received far too little attention, but it unfortunately does not fall within the scope of this book either. Here we are concerned with public investment projects in productive activities. We shall not directly cover, therefore, 'service' projects such as agricultural extension or technological research on the one hand, or 'non-productive' investments such as hospitals and schools on the other, although many of the techniques discussed will have a bearing on the treatment of these sorts of projects.

We have already made reference in passing to the leading 'textbooks' in the field, which are UN (1958), OECD (1968), UNIDO (1972) and IBRD (1975). For the applications to specific sectors, Adler (1971) on transport, Price-Gittinger (1972) on agriculture and OECD (1968) on industry are all useful. The British Ministry of Overseas Development 'manual' (ODM, 1972) contains a helpful set of 'checklists' of information required for project presentation, and King (1967) gives a description of various projects financed by the World Bank and their subsequent fate. Scott (1975) provides a number of useful examples of project appraisal in practice using the 'OECD' method. Finally, Hirschman (1967) is a short but very revealing account of the unforeseen factors that made for success or failure of some development projects around the world; Waterston (1965) examines this topic in the wider context of the experience of development planning as a whole; and Hanson (1965) explores it within the framework of public enterprise in developing economies.

CHAPTER 2

THE INVESTMENT CRITERION

INVESTMENT means the commitment of resources to the formation of capital assets, which in turn allows a stream of new resources to be generated in the future. The value of the capital asset created, in the form of plant or construction, depends upon the value of these future flows, and for the investment to be 'acceptable' then the value of the asset must exceed its cost. Thus the central aspects of investment analysis in the public sector are three: the forecasting of these flows over the life of the project; their valuation; and their reduction to a 'present value' which can be compared with present costs to form an 'investment criterion'. It follows, therefore, that the value of the capital asset depends upon the use to which it is to be put and the development of the rest of the economy over its life. In the private sector the profit expectations of the capitalist are the relevant measure, while in the public sector there is a wider economic standard; nevertheless, the methodology of the investment criterion (as opposed to the meaning of the parameters) is similar.

Cash and Resource Flows

The first step in investment appraisal is the establishment of the flows involved. Starting with the 'cash-flow' concept, the important idea is the convention that income and expenditure are only entered in the year in which a cash transaction actually takes place – whether receipts or payments. In consequence, concepts such as depreciation, sinking funds and net assets are not required. All expenditure appears as a negative item (outflow from the project) and income as a positive flow (inflow to the project) over the project life.

Let us examine the example of a sawmill project with an initial investment of 10 million pesos* and an operating life of ten years. Production costs are based on the output volume and plant maintenance, the latter (with administration expenses) totalling 1 million pesos a year, while the unit production costs are p. 200 per ton. The price of the timber produced is p. 350 per ton ex-factory, and the capacity of the sawmill is 20,000 tons per annum. In the table, we see the original investment cost in Year 0, the operating costs of p. 5 million (p. 1m. +p. $200 \times 20,000$) in Years 1 to 10, and the sales revenue (p. $350 \times 20,000$ = p. 7m.) in the same years. From these we derive the cash flow in each year, which turns from negative to positive. Note also that construction takes only one year, and full production starts the next.

SAWMILL PROJECT: CASH FLOWS (PESOS M.)

Year	Costs	Revenue	Cash flow
0	10.0	–	–10.0
1	5.0	7.0	2.0
2	5.0	7.0	2.0
3	5.0	7.0	2.0
4	5.0	7.0	2.0
5	5.0	7.0	2.0
6	5.0	7.0	2.0
7	5.0	7.0	2.0
8	5.0	7.0	2.0
9	5.0	7.0	2.0
10	5.0	7.0	2.0

Clearly, in practice the components of the cash flows will be much more complex than this but the four main elements are as follows:

(1) The investment cost, which must be broken down over the construction and installation period and is made up of

*This is not, of course, a real project: nor are the others in this book, although they are mostly based on the author's professional experience.

different elements such as site preparation, buildings, and equipment. These costs form the 'fixed assets' in the accounting sense.

(2) The operating costs, which will include labour (wages and salaries), raw materials (in this case wood lumber), spares for the plant, fuel and so on. These are conventionally divided into 'fixed' and 'variable' costs, the latter being dependent upon the volume of production (e.g. raw materials) and the latter upon the plant size (e.g. maintenance) and thus fixed for the project.

(3) The revenue, which depends upon the volume of sales (e.g. tons of timber) and their unit value, probably for a range of products and prices. Moreover, tax must be deducted on the basis of accounting profits.

(4) Finally, the 'life' of the project, after which the plant will be scrapped, which determines the period over which the cash flows are analysed. If appropriate, the sale value of the scrap itself and possibly the site are included.

Where the flows are 'economic', as opposed to 'financial' ones, they are usually termed 'costs and benefits' and include, as we have mentioned, effects outside those of the enterprise or project itself. For instance, an irrigation project would involve investment and operating costs in the same way as the previous example. However, in place of the 'revenue' item, we would have 'benefits' which might take the form of the increase in farmers' income in the area due to the increased water supply. The costs, for example, might be as follows: p. 20 million investment, spread over a two-year construction period, and maintenance costs equivalent to 1 per cent of the investment every year over the thirty-year life. The benefits might be an increase in land productivity of some p. 400 per hectare in annual output, for each of the 7000 hectares affected by the project. This gives us the cost–benefit flows in the table below.

IRRIGATION PROJECT: COST–BENEFIT FLOWS (PESOS M.)

Year	Costs	Benefits	Net flow
0	10.0	–	–10.0
1	10.0	–	–10.0
2	0.2	2.8	2.6
3	0.2	2.8	2.6
.	.	.	.
.	.	.	.
.	.	.	.
29	0.2	2.8	2.6
30	0.2	2.8	2.6
31	0.2	2.8	2.6

As can be seen, there is no essential arithmetic difference between the flow layouts for the financial and economic analyses, the real difference lying in the meaning of the figures.

Discounting and the Investment Decision

Having established the cash or cost–benefit flows (the estimation of the values is discussed in Chapter 2 below), these must be related to a common standard of comparison. This is done by *discounting* future flows to the present, on the basis of the following argument:

A hundred pesos, if invested in a bank, accumulates interest. If the rate of interest is 10 per cent, then the sum will be worth p. 110 after one year, p. 121 after two, p. 133 after three, and so on. p. 100 in the third year, therefore, is equivalent to the p. 75 (100 × 100 ÷ 133) that must be invested now to obtain that sum in three years' time–in other words, as far as the investor is concerned, an offer of p. 100 in three years' time is as attractive as an offer of p. 75 now.

This is the justification for discounting, which enables flows to be compared with one another in different years and with the present. The *discount factor* is the inverse of the compound interest formula for that year, and the flow for the year is multiplied by this to get the *present value*. Thus for the third year, the calculation in this case is

$$\text{Present Value} = \frac{100}{(1+0.1)^3} = \frac{100}{1.33} = 75$$

For a private enterprise, or a public corporation carrying out a financial analysis, the discount rate used is normally the interest rate at which bank loans are available, or in the case when the enterprise's own funds are used, the rate which banks would pay for the deposit of such funds – their 'opportunity cost' – the important point being that own funds are not 'free'. In the case of the public investment criterion, the discount rate is set by the central planning authority (see Part II) but is similarly related to the alternative use of the funds.

The formula for the Net Present Value of a project is the sum of the flow (x_i) in a particular year (i) from the initial year (0) to the last (n), discounted in the manner indicated above:

$$V = \frac{x_0}{(1+r)^0} + \frac{x_1}{(1+r)^1} + \ldots + \frac{x_n}{(1+r)^n} = \sum_{i=0}^{n} \frac{x_i}{(1+r)^i}$$

the 'acceptance criterion' being that the Net Present Value should be positive:

$$V > 0$$

We can also present this in separate parts, by discounting the benefits (B) and costs (C) individually, in which case the criterion becomes that the discounted benefits should exceed the discounted costs:

$$B > C$$
$$V = B - C > 0$$

The other important definition is that of the Internal Rate of Return, which is defined as that interest rate (R) for which the Net Present Value of the project is zero – the solution to the equation:

$$V = \sum_{i=0}^{n} \frac{x_i}{(1+R)^i} = 0$$

In this case the investment criterion is that the Internal Rate of Return should be greater than the discount rate:

$$R > r$$

Generally, we can state that for a single project, the following relationships hold:

when $V>0$ then $R>r$ and $B>C$
when $V=0$ then $R=r$ and $B=C$
when $V<0$ then $R<r$ and $B<C$

So that as far as a single project is concerned, the acceptance criteria of 'positive NPV' 'IRR greater than discount rate' and 'discounted benefits greater than discounted costs' are equivalent, and it is usual to present all three in the project appraisal report.

Taking the example of the sawmill discussed above, we can examine the calculation procedure. Suppose that a development bank is willing to lend to the firm at 8 per cent per annum. The discount factor for each year is found from tables such as those at the back of this volume and the cash flow is multiplied by this figure. The resulting total is the Net Present Value, and as in this case it is positive, the investment is judged worth while.

SAWMILL PROJECT: DISCOUNTED CASH FLOW

Year	Cash flow	Discount factor	Discounted cash flow
0	−10.00	1.000	−10.00
1	2.00	0.926	1.85
2	2.00	0.857	1.71
3	2.00	0.794	1.59
4	2.00	0.735	1.47
5	2.00	0.681	1.36
6	2.00	0.630	1.26
7	2.00	0.583	1.17
8	2.00	0.540	1.08
9	2.00	0.500	1.00
10	2.00	0.463	0.93

Net Present Value =   + 3.42

The procedure for an economic analysis is exactly the same. Taking the irrigation example again, we assume that the planning ministry has determined that a discount rate of 12 per cent should be applied, and calculate the discounted cash flows as before. The result is a negative Net Present Value, so that, other things being equal, the proposal should be turned down.

IRRIGATION PROJECT: DISCOUNTED COST–BENEFIT FLOWS

Year	Net flow	Discount factor	Discounted flow
1	−10.00	1.000	−10.00
2	−10.00	0.893	− 8.93
3	2.60	0.797	2.07
4	2.60	0.712	1.85
.	.	.	.
.	.	.	.
.	.	.	.
29	2.60	0.037	0.10
30	2.60	0.033	0.09
31	2.60	0.030	0.08

Net Present Value   − 0.23

Clearly, the higher the rate of interest, the more the future flows are discounted and thus the lower the Net Present Value that emerges from the calculations. Returning to the sawmill project, we use a range of interest rates to get both positive and negative NPVs as shown in the table. As can be seen, the NPV passes from positive to negative between the interest rates of 14 per cent and 16 per cent, so that the Internal Rate of Return must lie between these values.

SAWMILL PROJECT: DISCOUNT RATES AND NPVs

Discount rate per cent	Net Present Value
8	3.42
10	2 29
12	1.30
14	0.43
16	−0.33
18	−1.01

In practice, we can try more and more discount rates until a sufficiently accurate result is found. Alternatively, we can draw a graph of the relationship (Figure 1), the intersection with the horizontal axis giving the value of the IRR – about 15·1 per cent. This value is the solution ('root') of the equation for the Internal Rate of Return, and although a computer is normally used for calculations of any size, the method of numerical estimation is based on the same principle.

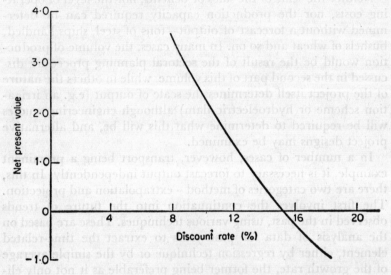

FIG. 1: Internal Rate of Return

These discounting techniques are central to the modern concept of investment appraisal and, as we have seen, are common to both financial and economic appraisal. The difference, as we have said before, lies in the meaning of the parameters themselves.

The Estimation of Parameter Values

We cannot, in so short a volume, enter fully into the complexity of the methods of establishing the parameter values in the flows we have been discussing. On the one hand, the methods depend to a great extent upon the sector being analysed, the country concerned and the nature of the project itself, while on the other this is as much a matter of practical experience in project planning as one of established rules. Moreover, the evaluation of the physical characteristics of the investment (i.e. construction work) is a matter for the design engineers, and the establishment of 'shadow prices' and 'external effects' are discussed in subsequent chapters. None the less, it would be appropriate and perhaps useful to mention here some of the more important aspects of parameter estimation as they effect the 'project economist' in an appraisal team.

Neither the scale of the sales or benefits, nor the level of operating costs, nor the production capacity required can be determined without a forecast of output – tons of steel, ships handled, bushels of wheat and so on. In many cases, the volume of production would be the result of the sectoral planning procedure discussed in the second part of this volume, while in others the nature of the project itself determines the scale of output (e.g. an irrigation scheme or hydroelectric dam) although engineering studies will be required to determine what this will be, and alternative project designs may be examined.

In a number of cases, however, transport being a prominent example, it is necessary to forecast output independently. In this, there are two categories of method – extrapolation and projection. The first involves the continuation into the future of trends observed in the past, using various techniques. These are based on the analysis of data for past years to extract the time-related element, either by regression technique or by the simple average of the growth rate, the former being preferable as it not only eliminates the 'random' element but also indicates the degree of variation about the average growth rate derived. This gives a forecast expressed as the percentage increase per annum which, although a very crude method which can lead to wildly unrealistic conclusions if carried forward too far, is very widely used for want of better. The alternative is to apply some form of projection model, where the volume of output is related to another economic variable, such as port traffic to import–export volume or potable water requirements to the growth in urbanised population. These models can become extremely complex, as when the traffic pattern over a road network is to be projected, and they can be distinguished from microplanning to the extent that they refer to the project alone and do not form part of an overall sectoral or national programme. In practice, these models form a whole subject apart, and some references to further reading are given in the Bibliography. In addition to the forecast trend in output, an indication of the expected probability of it occurring is also required – a topic to which we shall return.

An 'isolated' projection is necessarily based on a single variate: time. By taking a number of observations of the variable for previous years, of tourist arrivals (A) at a certain resort, for example, a relationship of the form (f) in terms of time (t)

$$A = f(t)$$

can be established. The crudest form is to take the average growth rate (a) from year to year, so that

$$a = \frac{1}{n} \sum_{t=1}^{n} \frac{A_t - A_{t-1}}{A_{t-1}}$$

and use this for future projections. A more sophisticated technique is to compute a regression equation* of the form:

$$\log A = \log B + a \log t$$

which will give the average growth rate (a) with a base value for traffic (B), a forecasting equation of the form:

$$A = B.t^a$$

and what is more, an estimate of the standard deviation in tourist traffic. Our tourist data might give an equation, for example:

$$A = 22.10^3.t^{0.083} \qquad \text{(standard deviation} = 0.011)$$

which would mean that with a trend value of 22,000 tourist arrivals at the beginning of the series, traffic has grown at an average rate of 8.3 per cent per annum, with a 95 per cent probability that the observations of the growth rate lie within a range of ± 2.2 percentage points of the mean value of 8.3 per cent. In consequence, if we assume that this trend will be continued in the future, then we expect growth to continue at 8.3 per cent, with the confidence intervals used either as 'high' and 'low' forecasts (of 10.5 and 6.1 per cent, respectively) directly, or indirectly as inputs to the sensitivity and probability analyses discussed in Chapter 7.

*See Yeomans (1968) vol. 1, chap. 6 and vol. 2, chap. 5.

It is evident that the extrapolation of a fixed rate of growth too far into the future produces ridiculous results – even in the example, to continue an 8 per cent growth rate over the next thirty years would result in a tenfold increase over the present level! In consequence, it is becoming common practice to set a 'saturation level' for the good or service in question, at which level it is felt that the market will cease to expand, or only very slowly. The estimated growth rate is then 'slowed down' steadily so as to produce a so-called S-curve (Figure 2) the degree of deceleration being determined by reference to previous examples elsewhere. In our tourism example, we might base the saturation level on the urban planners' judgment as to eventual hotel and beach space and on the unit absorptive capacity of comparable resorts in other countries, as well as the time taken to build up to this level. Another example might be the number of households with television sets which, after an initially high growth with the introduction of television broadcasting, will slow down and eventually reach a growth rate equivalent to that of the population (i.e. new households) when virtually all homes have one. In practice, this

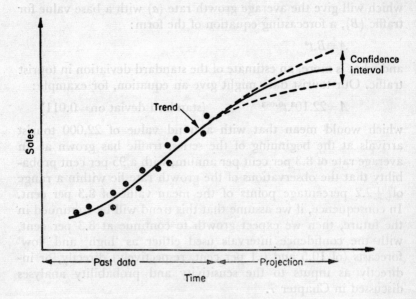

FIG. 2: The S-Curve

graphical form can be more simply expressed in terms of the rate of growth of demand, which rises and then falls over time (Figure 3). Calculation of the rates of growth of sales (in volume terms) in the past may well indicate that, in effect, the 'peak' has already been passed and a downward trend can be predicted with some confidence.

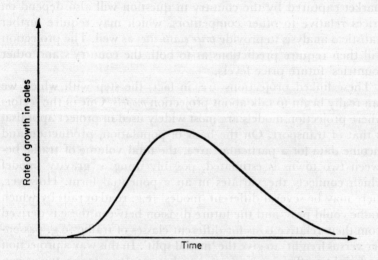

FIG. 3: Growth Rate in the S-Curve

A 'linked' projection is one where the variables we are interested in (such as the demand for tea exports) is linked to another variable (such as income growth in the industrialised countries) which is itself changing over time, and a forecast for which can be obtained. In the case where this latter variate is an important element in the domestic economy, then the forecast will be provided from the national planning system. The estimation equation might then take the form of a functional relationship, in this example, between world tea sales (A) and aggregate income in the OECD economies (Y):

$$\log A = \log B + a \log Y$$

This will have confidence intervals in the same way as in the previous example, but the key parameter (a) will not be the *trend* but the *elasticity*. The differentiation of the equation yields:

$$a = \frac{dA}{dY} \cdot \frac{Y}{A}$$

A forecast can then be obtained for OECD income (Y) from that institution itself, and applying the forecasting equation gives an estimate of total market size for the future. The share of this market captured by the country in question will also depend on prices relative to other competitors, which may require further statistical analysis to provide *price elasticities* as well. The projection will then require predictions as to both the country's and other countries' future price levels.

These linked projections are, in fact, the step with which we can really begin to talk about projection *models*. One of the sectors where projection models are most widely used in project appraisal is that of transport. On the basis of population, production and income data for a particular area, the total volume of traffic between two towns is estimated, possibly using a 'gravity' model which connects the variates in an exponential form. However, there may be several different 'modes' (e.g. road or rail) by which traffic could pass, and the future division between these is derived from their relative costs for different classes of traffic (e.g. passenger versus freight) to give the 'modal split'. In this way a projection for freight traffic on a railway line between two major towns can be generated, not as an extrapolation of past trends in traffic on that line, but as the result of a wider allocation exercise. Anticipated changes in both the railway (e.g. faster trains) and the competitive roads (e.g. shorter routes) which might alter either the total traffic between the towns or the modal split can also be included in such models. Where some of the variables of the model are under policy control, then the model may be used to evaluate alternative strategies – the main category of such optimisation models of interest to us being those concerned with investment allocation, to which we shall return in Chapter 10.

Having established the expected volume of output, the capacity needed can be derived, although a consideration of alternative project designs may imply an interaction between the two, especially where excess capacity or scale economies are involved – topics taken up in Part II. The estimation of the cost of the investment and the operating costs (on the basis of unit costs multiplied by the volume of production) is usually the responsibility of the design engineers, although the breakdowns required for the shadow-pricing exercise (see Chapters 4 and 5) may have to be calculated separately, because unit costs are usually based on the volume of work (e.g. dollars per cubic metre of earth moved in civil works) rather than on inputs (e.g. man-days) required, for investment costs, although the operating account is normally presented in more directly usable detail. Forecasting price levels for sales, particularly on international markets, is a difficult task and in practice involves as much judgment as analysis, so that again probability measures are relevant.

It is conventional in project appraisal reports to present costs, sales and benefits in terms of the price-level obtaining in the base year (Year 0). This does not mean that no price changes are anticipated, but rather that the overall level of inflation is expected to affect all prices more or less equally, having, so to speak, an equal impact on both sides of the present value equation. Where prices of particular items are expected to vary in a different way (e.g. oil), they should be forecast separately. The important thing to remember is that all assumptions should be clearly indicated, so that someone else reading the report can alter the estimates if required.

Finally, the project life is not just a matter of technical specification. With appropriate repair, most plant (whether equipment or construction) can have its life extended almost indefinitely, and in principle there is an 'optimal life' for plant, related to the relative costs of repair and replacement and closely connected to technological development. However, in practice, the exact life may not be very important in numerical terms, as by the date in question the flows are very heavily discounted. For example, raising the life of the sawmill project by one-fifth (i.e. from 10 to 12 years) would only raise the IRR from 15 per cent to 16 per cent. In cases where all the plant does not come to the end of its life at the same time, it is normal to include a 'residual value' for the ancillary equipment in the income flow for the final year of the project, usually a fraction of the appropriate investment cost based on the proportion of the useful life unexpired by that date. The land on which the factory is built does not 'wear out' so its full value is entered in the last year. In algebraic form, given a planning horizon (n years) and an equipment life (m years) the discounted residual value of an investment cost (K) is:

$$K \left\{ \frac{m-n}{m(1+r)^n} \right\}$$

and as land is considered as existing for ever $(m=\infty)$, the formula reduces in this case to:

$$K/(1+r)^n$$

and the same might be said of a facility such as a road-bed which, with appropriate maintenance, would effectively last for ever.

Suppose that the planning horizon for a project is 15 years, but equipment costing £16 million with a life of 25 years is installed as part of the investment. Unless an independent estimate for the 'scrap value' of the equipment depending on its age is available, as is the case for transport equipment where there is a good second-hand market, then the residual value (applying a 10 per cent discount rate) is given by:

$$16 \left\{ \frac{25-15}{25(1+0.1)^{15}} \right\} = 16 \times 0.4 \times 0.239 = £1.53 \text{ million}$$

This is then added to the Net Present Value.

Further Points

Here we shall comment on a few aspects of methodology which can be considered as 'refinements' and supply a short bibliography that will allow further reading on the topic of this chapter.

In the case where two alternative projects exist to achieve the same objective, but with different time-profiles of costs and benefits, then the NPV and IRR criteria may give different results as to which is preferable. Suppose Project A to have most of its costs in early years, while those of Project B are spread over a longer period: both projects having similar benefit flows but only one of the two is to be chosen. At low discount rates, A might be preferable to B (i.e. have a higher NPV), but as the rate is raised, B's costs are reduced more rapidly and at a certain point there is a 'crossover' after which B is preferable to A, and finally the intersection with the horizontal axis yields a higher IRR for B than for A as Figure 4 shows. The important point is, however, that where the correct discount rate lies below the 'crossover' rate, then the NPV and IRR investment criteria will give different results. In fact, the NPV criterion, representing as it does the cost of capital, is the correct measure, which is why the IRR, for all its simplicity, is not always a reliable indicator. In this case the NPV of *A* is greater than that of *B* at the planning discount rate (*r*), and thus *A* is preferable, even though *B* has a higher IRR than A. This case is not merely a hypothetical one; it occurs

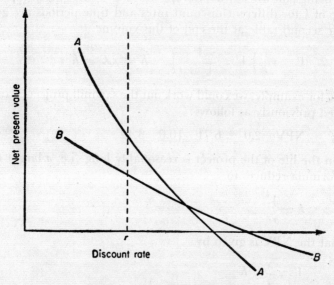

FIG. 4: Alternative Projects

quite frequently where there is an alternative between a 'technology' involving heavy initial investment and low running costs, and one with the converse characteristics. A good example is the choice between thermal and hydroelectric plant to generate a certain amount of electricity, the former involving relatively low investment but high operating costs (fuel oil) and the latter considerable investment (dams) but very little operating costs. The higher the discount rate, the less attractive the hydroelectric alternative becomes.

The discounting formulation itself can be reduced to a simple form that is useful both for analysis and for 'back of the envelope' calculations in the field. Let us assume that the investment flow

(K) takes place in one year (0), and that the net flows subsequent years (x_i) are equal, in which case the NPV can be represented as

$$V = \sum_{i=1}^{n} \frac{x_i}{(1+r)^i} - K$$

which can be further reduced to the form below, the main expression being known as the Compound Discount Factor (k). The value of k for different discount rates and time periods are given in the second table at the end of this volume.

$$V = x \frac{1}{r} \left\{ 1 - \frac{1}{(1+r)^n} \right\} - K = x.k - K$$

Thus, for example, we could work out the sawmill project example quoted previously as follows:

$$\text{NPV} = 2.0 \times 6.71 - 10.0 = 3.42$$

When the life of the project is reasonably long (i.e. n large) then the formula reduces to

$$k \simeq \frac{1}{r}$$

so that the NPV is given by

$$V \simeq \frac{x}{r} - K$$

and the IRR by

$$R \simeq \frac{x}{K}$$

This not only demonstrates the formal equivalence of the NPV and IRR criteria in the case of a single project ($V>0$ when $R>r$) but also provides a rapid method for rough calculations of these results.

Finally, some further reading. On project presentation, we have already cited some texts, but for books specialising on the investment criterion, see OECD (1968, vol. I) and Merrett and Sykes (1963), while Millward (1971) explores the 'public economics' side of the problem. Wolfe (1966) has a good discussion on the forecasting of the flows, while Yeomans (1968) provides an introduction to the statistical background. On projection methods, UN (1958) gives some very good practical techniques, while Theil (1971) contains a full theoretical treatment. Although related to British industrial practice, Turner (1974) contains some useful advice on forecasting which can, with care, be applied to a developing economy. However, there does not appear to be any book available on forecasting for development projects, which is unfortunate as this aspect of investment appraisal is one upon which much of the reliability of the feasibility study will depend. On some more theoretical aspects of the investment decision itself, see Hirschliefer (1968) and lastly, on the 'hydro versus thermal' analysis, there is a full treatment in Van der Tak (1967).

CHAPTER 3

SECONDARY COSTS AND BENEFITS

THE definition and estimation of the external costs and benefits of an investment are central to the concept of 'economic' or 'social' project appraisal, as opposed to a purely 'financial' or 'private' one. Indeed, this is the aspect which underlines the need for a separate method of investment evaluation, and is part of the justification for public investment itself. We can distinguish between two broad categories of external effect caused by a project. First, there are the significant effects upon the immediate 'vicinity' of the project – the spatially proximate area, closely related production sectors or the rest of an investment programme. These are usually known as 'secondary' costs and benefits, and sometimes as 'indirect' ones, as opposed to the 'primary' or 'direct' value of the project in itself. Second, there are the effects that have a marginal impact on the economy as a whole, which are taken up through the use of shadow pricing, discussed in Chapters 4 and 5 below. There is some theoretical difficulty in defining the boundaries between these two categories, because the classifications depend upon the case in hand and are as much a matter of pragmatic judgement as of economic principle. Thus the definition of the project itself might well have to be extended to cover the major secondary effects (e.g. from the dam itself to the river valley as a whole), and the extent to which the impact is 'followed through' will depend upon the scale of such effects relative to the other elements in the appraisal.

In consequence, no strict methodology can be laid down for the estimation of secondary costs and benefits, and here we shall mainly proceed by example. None the less, we can treat four topics separately – the economic impact upon the immediate vicinity, the effect upon local markets, the consequences for linked production sectors and the influence upon the rest of a public investment programme.

Immediate Local Impact

It is quite common for large infrastructure projects to have an important economic impact on their immediate vicinity which is not the direct aim of the investment itself. Of course, many are designed to do just that, such as an irrigation scheme planned to increase crop yields, but in these cases the scope of the project is defined to cover this part of the production process too, and the net value of the output increment becomes a *direct* benefit of the project, as we have seen in the previous chapter. There is a large class of projects, however, where apart from the primary purpose of the investment there are important secondary costs and benefits that must be taken into account.

The method for calculating these secondary costs and benefits is essentially the same as that for the primary effect: to calculate their annual values over the life of the project and discount them to the present. This additional net present value (positive or negative) is then added to the NPV of the project. The main problem lies in the estimation of the volume and value of these effects, particularly since they are outside the direct control of the project agency itself. This involves, therefore, a considerable degree of guesswork, and the assumptions must be presented clearly in the project report so that they can be subsequently varied if required. The main object is to estimate how much higher (or lower) the incomes of those persons or enterprises in the project area are as a consequence of the project than they would otherwise have been. This, in turn, requires a 'miniature' appraisal of production activities in the area, although not in so much detail as for the project proper. The technical aspects of the impact (e.g. the area flooded by a proposed hydroelectric barrage) are usually estimated by qualified experts (e.g. hydrologists) but the economic implications must be derived on an *ad hoc* basis, employing the methods of the previous chapter and applying shadow pricing as well if appropriate.

Let us take the case of a hydroelectric project, the water reservoir for which will result in the flooding of a considerable arable area of the valley upstream from the barrage. The area affected is some 1000 hectares of land presently under peasant cultivation of maize. We estimate the present average income per hectare on the basis of maize yields, the price of maize, and the cost of inputs, so as to find the net income per hectare (x) which in this case comes to $ 50 a year. If this were to be maintained constant over the project life, then we could calculate the net present value of this income stream (X), which is in fact the opportunity cost of the land flooded. Taking, say, a 12 per cent discount rate and a project life of 50 years, we would have*

$$X = 8{\cdot}304x = \$\ 415 \text{ per hectare}$$

Refinements to this simple calculation might include the upward adjustment for growth in agricultural productivity in the area had the flooding not occurred and the positive benefits from, say, fishing in the reservoir, although this latter could only be counted if it were not possible to do the same in any case. However, taking the valuation as worked out, the loss of 1000 hectares would mean a total cost of $ 0·42 million to be added to the direct costs (construction and operation) and benefits (power generated) of the hydroelectric project itself:

HYDROELECTRIC PROJECT

Item	Nature	$m.
Primary benefits:	Power sales	5·00
Primary costs:	Construction, operation	4·00
Primary Net Present Value		1·00
Secondary costs:	Inundation	0·42
Total Project Present Value		0·58

Price Effects upon Local Market

Quite commonly the consequence of a project is to change prices on local markets, the most relevant and most frequently analysed case being where an increase in supply or a reduction in supply costs results in a fall in market prices. Clearly, if the benefits to the consumer of such a price fall are not included, then the full

*Using the 'compound discount factor' formula from the previous chapter and the table at the end of the book.

value of the project is not being taken into account. For example, if increased supply of cement leads to a lower market price in a certain region, then this would represent foregone income to the producer, but there is an equal and opposite gain to the cement user, which should be included in an overall cost–benefit analysis. When this fall in price represents a saving to the user, *without* an increase in usage, then the effect is easily calculated. However, a fall in price will generally increase demand, and the saving to new users must be included.

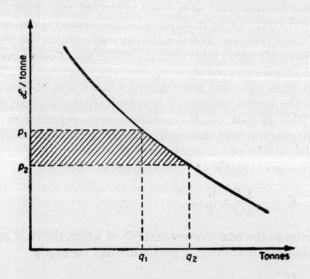

FIG. 5: Consumer Surplus

Thus, in terms of Figure 5, we have not only the savings on existing demand,

$$(p_1 - p_2) q_1$$

but also the 'triangle' which represents the savings to new units of demand that would be bought at prices between p_1 and p_2:

$$\tfrac{1}{2}(p_1 - p_2)(q_2 - q_1)$$

the whole being known* as the 'increase in consumer surplus':

$$(p_1 - p_2) q_1 + \tfrac{1}{2}(p_1 - p_2)(q_2 - q_1) = \tfrac{1}{2}(p_1 - p_2)(q_1 + q_2)$$

*For a detailed technical and theoretical discussion of this in the public investment context, see Millward (1971).

Of course the effect of, say, purchase of local inputs in driving *up* local prices should also be accounted for – but this is normally of little consequence.

A typical example, and one that is central to transportation planning, is that of a road project which reduces the cost of transport between two points, either by building a new (and more direct) route or by improving the road surface. As a result of the shortened distance or better traffic conditions, the cost for that 'stretch' is reduced – in terms of running (say) a typical bus, car or truck over the new road as opposed to the old one – from c_1 to c_2. These unit costs can be multiplied by the annual traffic level in each of these classes to find the annual traffic costs. The relevant comparison, of course, is between the traffic as it would have been (t_1), and as it is expected to be (t_2) with the improvement. Therefore two traffic forecasts are required – 'with' and 'without' the project. The normal procedure is to forecast the 'without' traffic on the basis of past trends, combined with expectations as to future population and economic activity in the area, and then derive the 'with' traffic on the basis of an 'elasticity' formula which relates changes in traffic (ΔT) to changes in costs (ΔC):

$$E = -\frac{\Delta T}{\Delta C} \cdot \frac{C}{T}$$

This relates to the *total* journey cost (C) of which the road project in question may form only a part, although naturally

$$\Delta C = c_2 - c_1$$

Moreover, it is conventional to assume that the value of the elasticity (E) is unity, so that the proportional increase in traffic is the same as the proportional decrease in costs:

$$\frac{t_2 - t_1}{t_1} = \frac{c_1 - c_2}{C}$$

and from there we proceed as before, the benefits being

$$X = \tfrac{1}{2}(c_1 - c_2)(t_1 + t_2)$$

A numerical example might clarify this. Suppose that the 'without' forecast for a particular year is 50,000 vehicles per annum passing along a certain stretch of road, the upgrading of which reduces transit costs for each vehicle along that stretch from 5 rupees to 3, a saving of 2 rupees on the average *overall* journey cost of 20 rupees. This 10 per cent saving in journey cost is translated into a 10 per cent expansion in traffic for the 'with' over the 'without' level. The benefits can then be calculated as

$$\tfrac{1}{2}(5-3)(50,000+55,000)=105,000 \text{ rupees}$$

It should be noted, in passing, that the greater part (some 100,000 rupees) of the benefits are cost savings to the existing traffic, so that the result is not highly sensitive to the value of the elasticity. Once calculated for each year, the benefits are discounted to the present for comparison with the investment cost and the difference in discounted maintenance costs between the new and old roads. This might yield:

ROAD IMPROVEMENT PROJECT

	Rupees (m.)
Investment costs	0.73
Increased maintenance	0.55
	1.28
Discounted benefits	1.82
Net Present Value of Project	+0·54

The Impact on Other Production Sectors

Possibly the most important externality of a project in the context of economic development is the stimulus given to production and investment in other sectors of the economy. It is difficult to be precise about this, but two general points can be made. First, that 'economic development' as a concept meaning more than just increases in national income, must involve the integration of the production structure. Although we shall deal with this under 'sectoral planning' in Part II, the evaluation of the impact upon other sectors is also a matter of project appraisal, especially where a non-marginal change is induced elsewhere in the economy that is too large to be handled within the shadow-pricing framework and too small to be considered as modifying the aggregate economic plan. Second, that we are generally considering the effect of the supply of a service or a commodity that was not freely available before, or the establishment of a market for a product constrained in its production by lack of one. In both cases, we are analysing the 'liberation' of production otherwise held back.

What we are trying to do in practice, then, is to measure the costs and benefits accruing to the sectors affected, and to add these (once discounted) to the NPV of the project as it stands. As in the case of the local impact studies we have just discussed, this is as much a matter of judgement as of established method, but the sources of information are somewhat different. Whereas in the case of the local impact study the project area can be examined directly by the project team, in the case of 'linkage' impact studies they must rely upon data sources such as censuses of production, sample enterprise accounts and ministerial surveys. What we are looking for are cases of production that is only made possible by the linkage with the public investment project.

Let us take as an example the establishment of a fishmeal processing plant to produce chicken feed. This will purchase considerable quantities of fish from the fisheries sector, and the extra income generated for fishermen (the difference between the purchase price and the cost of production) is a secondary benefit to be attributed to the project. The distribution of the benefit between secondary and primary categories will depend on the price paid in the transaction, but this is a matter of income distribution rather than economic value. For example, we might carry out a miniature cost–benefit analysis of fishing, based on the latest figures from the Economic Census and the Ministry of Agriculture for costs of production for that activity. We assume that the 50,000 tons of fish required per annum can be met by an expansion by 20 per cent of the present annual catch of 0·25 million tons. The costs of production for this latter total are estimated at some 280 million pesos a year by the sources mentioned, which gives us an average cost of some 1,120 pesos per ton: when this is set against a purchase price of 2000 pesos and scaled up by the tonnage required, it gives us a benefit to fishermen, in the form of profits, of 44 million pesos.* Against this we must set any extra investment required in the fisheries sector. The capital cost of vessels has presumably been included in the production cost, but some expansion in facilities (e.g. repair yards, storage sheds and

*That is $(2000-1120) \times 50,000 = 44$ million.

transport) may be needed at, say, an extra cost of 100 million pesos. This now enables us to calculate the total project value along with the direct costs and benefits. In this example the effect of including secondary benefits is to raise the internal rate of return from the somewhat meagre 11 per cent, on the basis of the direct costs and benefits, to a somewhat more substantial 15 per cent for the project as a whole.

FISHMEAL PLANT PROJECT

	Pesos (m.)	
Direct benefits	2130	
Direct costs	1590	
		540
Secondary benefits*	335	
Secondary costs	100	
		235
Net Present Value		775

On the output side (that is the public provision of inputs to other sectors), it is not always so easy to identify the benefits, except where, as in the case of rural electrification, the use of the product is limited to a narrow range of economic activities. Otherwise the benefits are usually implicit in the sectoral planning system, which should programme *output* in 'constraining' branches in line with the overall development of the economy rather than on the basis of attempts to calculate the marginal external benefits.

Effect upon the Rest of the Public Investment Budget

The last of the major categories is also closely related to the matters we shall take up again in Part II, but here we shall consider the marginal effect of a particular project upon the rest of an established capital expenditure programme in the public sector. The timing or location of a particular project may require a greater or lesser investment in other public projects than would otherwise be the case, and this must clearly be included in a full cost–benefit analysis. Moreover, as these costs and benefits usually

*That is, 44 million for 15 years' plant life, discounted at 10 per cent: $44 \times 7.606 = 335$.

happen to accrue to administrative agencies other than that directly concerned with the project, the result may well be of crucial interest to the central planner if not to the project analyst himself. There is some justification, therefore, for the treatment of this effect separately.

Again, the identification of these effects is a matter of judgement, particularly as to 'what would happen otherwise'. The extent of the modifications in the other public investment programmes identified will also depend upon the degree of integration in the planning system itself – that is, whether they have already been worked out and included in the final plan or not. In any case, they must be separated out.

Two specific examples of importance may make this clearer. First, where extra expenditure elsewhere is engendered by the project, and the second where the scheduling of another project is altered by this one. The first occurs where, say, the development of a mining complex by the Ministry of Natural Resources requires that the Ministry of Transport construct improved roads and bridges to carry the heavy vehicles involved. The cost of upgrading these roads (over and above any regrading that might be necessary anyway) must be attributed to the project as part of its total cost, even though it is part of the expenditure programme of another administrative agency. The second occurs when the implementation of the project requires that other projects be brought forward or allows them to be postponed. The benefit (or cost) is simply the difference between the discounted value of the other project in the 'with' and 'without' cases. An example might be the decision to develop a beach resort for foreign tourists, the expansion planned in hotel capacity being such as to require an extension of the local airport so as to take international flights carrying tourists that previously had been routed via the main metropolitan airport. In consequence, traffic at this latter airport will be lower than forecast, the planned extension there (at a cost of £10 million) can be delayed by two years – from 1981 to 1983 – the difference in the dates at which capacity operation is expected to be reached. Thus we must compare the net present cost (discounted, say, at 12 per cent to the present, 1977) of the two alternatives, the difference (£1·3 million) being the net benefit attributable to the tourism project, to be set against the cost of amplifying the local airport.

RESCHEDULING OF MAIN AIRPORT EXTENSION

	Capital Cost (£m.)	Discount Factor	Discounted Cost (£m.)
Extension in 1981	10.0	0.636	6.4
Extension in 1983	10.0	0.507	5.1
Difference	—		1.3

Further Points

The main problem in evaluating secondary costs and benefits, as we have seen, is that while they are in some sense 'the very stuff of development' they are notoriously hard to pin down in any general way even though they are usually strikingly obvious in specific cases. For this reason they tend to gather an honourable mention in discussions of planning but little more, despite their importance. This is perhaps unfortunate, because one of the crucial reasons for concentrating on project appraisal rather than central planning or reliance on commercial criteria is the existence of externalities.

One class of external effects that might have been considered in this chapter is that sometimes known as 'intangibles'. By this we mean not just those project outputs that cannot be quantified in economic terms (such as health or public order) but which are direct aims of projects and part of a planning process, but also the social or environmental impact of a particular public investment. The example of the noise caused by a major airport is a good one, and also of a fairly unambiguous nature. An attempt to examine this sort of 'environmental cost' can be made through the comparison of real estate values in areas only otherwise differentiated by the noise level, the difference between the total capital value of the area round the airport and a similar 'quiet' area being a net secondary disbenefit attributable to a project. However, this sort of methodology is a extremely limited in scope of application, and certainly cannot hope to evaluate social effects such as the impact of a major road through slums or that of hotels on coastal communities. These are impossible to value in economic terms by definition, so that there is no purpose in searching for a methodology. This does not mean, however, that these should be ignored, rather the opposite: when serious social costs are anticipated, an effort should be made to evaluate the 'next best' alternative in economic terms that will avoid the social costs, and explicitly present the alternatives to the authorities. In this way the social and economic costs can be balanced in a logical manner.

Reading on secondary costs and benefits is sparse. However, on the immediate local impact of large water schemes, see Krutilla and Eckstein (1958), and for the consumer surplus analysis as applied to transport projects, Adler (1971). The Prest and Turvey (1965) survey covers the theoretical debate on externalities and compensation criteria quite well, while Hirschman (1967) and King (1967) discuss the practical problems involved in a number of large infrastructure projects financed by the World Bank. Finally, for an excellent analysis of the effect of rural electrification on small-scale irrigation see Lal (1972).

CHAPTER 4

THE ECONOMIC VALUATION OF COMMODITIES

To the extent that the effect of a project extends beyond the 'secondary' impact discussed in the previous chapter, and the market prices of the goods and services used in or produced by the project are inadequate indicators of their value to the economy as a whole, some different system of evaluating the inputs and outputs must be established. The inefficiency of market prices as indicators of value cannot be fully discussed here* without entering into neo-classical equilibrium theory, but high tariff barriers, an opportunity cost of labour below the market wage, shortages of public capital funds, monopoly profits, foreign exchange constraints and administered prices for basic products are all contributory factors. There is a need, therefore, for a more objective basis upon which to base commodity valuation for the purposes of project appraisal.

The use of the term 'shadow prices' in this context can be somewhat confusing, particularly since the term originated in the field of linear programming. Although in theory (see Part II) the mathematical programming approach to planning might be used to calculate 'optimal' prices for project use in a planned economy, this is not what the term has come to mean, in fact rather the opposite: it is seen as part of a method of separating the project from the plan and valuing it independently, as far as is possible in a distorted economy. Terms such as 'accounting prices' and 'efficiency prices' have been proposed as alternatives, but these also have inappropriate overtones, so that the most common form remains 'shadow prices'.

*For a good explanation see the opening chapters of Little and Mirrlees (1974)

In this chapter we shall examine the important recent development in commodity valuation: the application of international prices to 'traded' goods, and its limitations preceded by an explanation of the practice of 'netting out' of income to the state, such as taxation.

The Treatment of State Income

The first and perhaps most comprehensible adjustment to market prices is that arising from the incidence of indirect taxation. If the market price of an input used on a project contains tax, then this will raise the price above the cost of the resources involved in its production, and thus to find the opportunity cost to the community as a whole we must take the pre-tax price – the 'shadow' price in this case. For example, if gasoline purchased for a project is sold (or, as in the illustration below, is used by the beneficiaries of a project) at 5 pesos per litre retail, but bears a 100 per cent tax, then the real resource cost would have been p. 2.5, and this is the appropriate cost to enter in the calculation: 50 per cent of the market price. Another way of expressing the same concept would be to add the tax element in the expenditure directly to the NPV of the project as an external benefit – an addition to state income – but it is conventional to calculate the shadow price in the way we have indicated.

The same consideration applies to the net profit component in the goods and services supplied by state enterprise, which should be deducted from the unit cost of inputs to the project because in economic (although not administrative) terms it is exactly equivalent to a sales tax. Equally, the subsidy or state enterprise loss element in any particular input price should be *added* to the project costs, as it is equivalent to a 'negative' tax.

This adjustment may be of some considerable importance. For example, the upgrading of a road from gravel to asphalt would involve a reduction in user costs, taking the form of reduced vehicle operating expenses. The table shows the calculation of opportunity costs from the market price of vehicle operations. The new road surface will reduce these costs by 20 per cent (for the 50,000 vehicles using the stretch of road each year), but the valuation at market prices overestimates the benefits (i.e. cost reduction) by about one-third.

BENEFITS OF ROAD IMPROVEMENT

	Market price	Tax content	Opportunity cost
Unit operating cost (c/km):			
Fuel, lubricants	20	10	10
Equipment, spares	10	4	6
Driver, maintenance	20	0	20
Total	50	14	36
Annual costs ($ per annum):			
Total	25,000		18,000
Saving	5,000		3,600

The shadow price of road transport, in this case (and leaving aside the other adjustments discussed below) would therefore be 72 per cent of the market price. In evaluating, say, transport costs in a large construction project this ratio could also be applied to the total expenditure under the 'road transport' head to provide an estimate of the opportunity cost. With indirect taxation accounting for as much as a sixth of national income in developing countries, the effect can be considerable.

The Shadow Price of Traded Goods

The major innovation in the shadow pricing methodology in recent years has been the valuation of 'traded' goods at 'border prices'. The argument runs as follows. A large number of goods and services used in projects or produced by them are either imported or exported by the country in question, so that the effect of using more of these goods or producing more of them has a direct effect on the external trade position. For example, if wheat is freely imported for domestic consumption to make up production shortfalls, then the effect of a project to produce more wheat is to reduce the import bill and thus save foreign exchange. It follows, then, that in these cases the true economic value of the output is its c.i.f. import price – known as the 'border price' – whatever the domestic market price (probably arbitrarily set by the government) may be. This concept also applies to exported goods to the extent that project output increases them, or uses inputs that might otherwise have been exported. The effect may, of course, be indirect: an input to a project may be a local product, the limited supply of which then requires that imports be increased for other uses.

The border price is, quite simply, the c.i.f. import or f.o.b. export price, if the good in question is freely available from, or saleable onto, international markets. In other words, the marginal foreign exchange revenue or expenditure. In the case, therefore, where a change in import or export volume would affect the world price, this should be taken into account. The establishment of the correct border price is not usually a problem, as it can be established either from engineering data (e.g. turbines for a hydroelectric plant) or indirectly from customs statistics.

Traded goods, then, should be valued at international prices. However, these will be expressed, so to speak, in dollars rather than pesos, and represent a certain sum of scarce foreign exchange. To the extent that domestic prices are higher than the international level when converted at the official exchange rate, due to the tariff protection on imports, we cannot simply convert border prices into local currency to be compared with the other items in the net present value of the project; we must either convert these latter to an international price-equivalent or convert the former to the domestic price-equivalent. If, say, on average local prices are 20 per cent above the international level, this means that at an official exchange rate of Rs. 10 to the US$, a thousand dollars' worth of imported goods at c.i.f. prices will, on average, sell for Rs. 12,000 on the domestic market; thus, to the domestic consumer, one US $ is worth Rs. 12.*

To handle this problem, the 'OECD manual' (OECD, 1968) suggests that *all* inputs and outputs should be valued at international prices multiplied by the official exchange rate, while the 'UNIDO manual' (UNIDO, 1972) suggests a similar method, except that the international prices be converted to the domestic price level by multiplying with a 'shadow exchange rate', itself the ratio of domestic to international prices. The two methods are equivalent, then, except that the former will give

*This ratio of 1.2:1 (=83%) is known as the 'standard conversion factor' in the OECD method, and its inverse (120%) is the 'shadow exchange rate' of the UNIDO method. See Scott (1974) for an excellent comparative discussion of these and other methods of allowing for the high opportunity cost of foreign exchange.

values consistently lower than the latter by a constant ratio, although the investment decision criterion of 'net present value greater than zero' and the value of the internal rate of return will be unaffected.

As an example of the OECD method, take domestic textile production from domestically produced yarn, both commodities being traded. The market price of plain cotton cloth is Rs 5 per metre, but there is a 25 per cent duty on imported cloth and imports only cost the economy the import price of Rs 4. Cotton yarn is exported, but this also is taxed, the export price being 40 per cent above the local price received by the exporter (Rs 3.50 per metre) after the tax has been paid. Adjustment of the 'other' input cost component is made here by multiplying by the ratio of international to domestic prices (1 : 1.2), although we could calculate the shadow prices of the items (e.g. labour, equipment, etc.) separately. Comparison of the profit margin 'surplus' at shadow prices and market prices then indicates that although the production of cotton cloth yields a profit to the manufacturer of Rs 1.00 per yard, it leads to a net *loss* to the economy as a whole of Rs 0.75 a yard, mainly due to the existence of a comparatively high price for yarn as compared to cloth on the international markets, possibly indicating that other countries have narrower manufacturing margins.

UNIT VALUES IN CLOTH PRODUCTION (RUPEES PER YARD)

	Market prices	Shadow prices
Input costs:		
Yarn	2.50	3.50
Other	1.50	1.25
	4.00	4.75
Output value	5.00	4.00
Surplus	+1.00	−0.75

This application of international prices to traded goods does *not* necessarily imply a commitment to the principles of a policy of 'free trade', but rather a recognition of the opportunities available at the margin to an economy exposed to international markets –

these, for all their bias against the Third World, must be taken as given. In the example just given it was shown that at the margin greater cotton yarn exports would have been more desirable than continued import-substitution for cloth. This does not mean that the industry as a whole should be dismantled, as many other factors play a part in deciding upon an industrialisation strategy – all it shows is that in the short run there is a net cost to the economy. A serious problem does arise, however, as we shall see shortly, in the determination of which commodities are to be considered as traded, but once this is decided, then the method described is analytically correct. It is, in fact, an important step in the separation of projects from central plans in the planning process.

We have, in effect, defined 'traded goods' as those commodities which are actually imported or exported, to which we would include those which may not actually be but which could be traded without any special administrative decision. In a particular country there may exist, however, a number of commodities the import of which is forbidden: so that the dividing line between traded and non-traded goods will depend upon government policy as well as upon the intrinsic nature of some of them (e.g. water, power) which makes them normally non-traded. Steel, for example, is a good freely available on international markets, but many countries ban the import of basic steel products – covering the whole of domestic requirements from domestic steel-mills – in which case steel becomes *de facto* non-traded. Although, of course, a critique of the short-term 'efficiency' of such a decision could be based on the principles of comparative advantage by comparing the domestic cost of production of steel (at international price-equivalents) with the import price, once a strategic decision *has* been made then the methodology for non-traded goods must inevitably be applied. The borderline for definition of 'traded' will depend, then, on the development strategy of the country concerned, which will in turn derive from political as well as economic objectives and may well change over time as the economy matures.

The Valuation of Non-traded Commodities

Non-traded commodities include, naturally, goods and services which are not normally traded internationally anyway, such as electricity or transport services.* No international price can therefore be found for these commodities. In the case where these are a relatively unimportant element of the project costs a 'standard conversion factor' can be used, which relates average domestic to average international prices, but when non-traded inputs occur as significant items (such as road user costs in a road project) then the item is broken down into its own input components (i.e. the resources required to produce it) and the shadow price of each of these components applied so the 'true' cost can be found. Taking once again as an example road user costs: these would be broken down into (say) fuel, labour and equipment. These would in turn be adjusted for taxation, the shadow wage rate (see Chapter 5), the import price of automotive equipment, and the costs (at border prices) of refining imported petroleum into gasoline. This may be quite a complicated procedure, and possibly requires the use of input–output techniques to establish the 'final' inputs (traded goods and factors inputs) required for the eventual production of non-traded commodities. It is not, however, a task which need be carried out by the project analyst on each occasion: the shadow price (or rather, the ratio of this to the market price) of the commodity (e.g. road transport) can be estimated periodically by the central planning agency and issued to the operating agencies evaluating projects.

As an illustration, we can return to the figures from the 'road regrading' example discussed above, and the supposed cost breakdowns are shown in the table below. The tax component we have seen before – this is netted off. Imports are both direct (automotive equipment) and indirect (gasoline), and are valued at the border price. The 'profit' item in the table is the marginal economic surplus in the state refinery, which is also netted off as a cost (i.e. it forms an addition to the net benefits of the project) in this calculation. Finally, labour is involved both directly in the transport itself (i.e. drivers) and indirectly in the inputs (i.e. refining, maintenance), so a shadow wage-rate ratio (80 per cent) is applied to the employment costs. In sum, these adjustments give an overall shadow price of 31 cents per kilometre, equivalent to 62 per cent of the market price. In practice, we would calculate

*Although in the case of contiguous countries, even these might be traded, but this is uncommon.

this for different types of vehicles and road surfaces, calculating a shadow price ratio for each category using a standard unit of measurement such as 'cents per ton-kilometre' and then combining these in a weighted average. This could then be issued by, say, the planning section of the ministry of transport – classified according to road categories (motorway, tarmac, gravel, earth, etc.) and vehicle type (car, bus, truck, etc.) – to the operating agencies responsible for carrying out the project appraisal.

SHADOW PRICE OF ROAD TRANSPORT (c/km)

	Tax	Imports	Profit	Labour	Total unit cost
Market prices:					
Fuel, lubricants	10	7	2	1	20
Equipment, spares	4	6	0	0	10
Maintenance, driver etc.	0	5	0	15	20
Total market unit cost	14	18	2	16	50
Shadow price ratios	0	1.0	0	0·8	—
Shadow cost	0	18	0	13	31

The problem of valuing non-traded goods when they are *outputs* is a much more difficult one. The market price of, say, electricity is set by the government in relation to the costs of production, and cannot be related directly to any 'objective' standard of value. Indeed, it is usually the case that there are many more persons and enterprises willing to consume electricity at the going price than those connected to the supply system. We can find its *cost* as an input to another project, by the method just described, but not its value as such in a power generation project. In a few cases, such as irrigation water, which is itself untraded but where we can find the (traded) value of the crops produced, the value of a non-traded good can be determined, but the use of the product is usually not specific enough for this and in any case is really equivalent to the redefinition of the 'output' of the project (i.e. crops rather than water) to make it traded. This difficulty is compounded by the fact that in most 'mixed' economies the bulk of public sector investment is in 'infrastructure' –

either physical infrastructure such as roads and dams or economic infrastructure such as steel and cement – while state intervention in a particular production branch is often accompanied by the strategic decision to end imports of that product, so that much of the output of public investment projects is non-traded.

The difficulty of valuing non-traded output would seem, then, to indicate that we have reached something of an impasse. In fact this blind alley is, so to speak, the result of having taken the wrong turning in the first place. The attempt to separate project analysis from central planning, especially that of sectoral production, fails when the project cannot be evaluated 'at the margin' by using border prices. The solution is not to continue searching for a shadow price, but to recognise that direct output planning is required within a wider framework – the topic of the second part of this book. In consequence, non-traded output targets can only be set from outside the project, and the project analysis itself is concerned with the establishment of the minimum-cost variant, all the inputs being analysed in the manner discussed above.

Further Points

The use of shadow prices, and their estimation in terms of international markets, has perhaps been the major advance in the methodological debate over project appraisal in recent years, but it has now gained fairly widespread acceptance. The best exposition is to be found in OECD (1968), continued by the same authors in Little and Mirrless (1974), an interesting debate on the topic being contained in BOUIES (1972). A difficulty of Little and Mirrlees's own *application* of their method is that they assert that all goods that *can* be traded ('tradables') should be treated as such–a commitment to the principles of free trade that is unacceptable to many countries. A similar approach to ours is given in UNIDO (1972), but here the domestic price level is used as the standard, with the international prices of traded goods being multiplied by a 'shadow exchange rate' set at the ratio between international and domestic prices. This is, in fact, the inverse of the OECD 'standard conversion factor'. A good presentation of the equivalence of these approach is given by Dasgupta in BOUIES (1972). For useful examples of shadow price calculations in practice, see Little and Scott (1976). The point on the difficulty of evaluating non-traded output is pursued further in FitzGerald (1977).

Another approach to shadow pricing that we have not discussed is that of 'equilibrium prices', which are defined as the prices that would have obtained were a 'free market' to obtain, although it is difficult to see what meaning these would have in a structurally distorted economic structure, let alone how they would be estimated. However, the proposal can be found in Harberger (1972), and is often supported – at least in theory – by other 'market' economists.

Finally, it should be pointed out that the concentration of academic interest and controversy on the issue of shadow prices can lead to an overemphasis on their importance within the process of project analysis as a whole. This imbalance is exacerbated in an inflationary situation or where the economic equilibrium is changing rapidly, because the exact (albeit relative) values of the shadow prices are themselves based on the shifting sand of market prices. There would seem to be, therefore, a strong argument for the use of approximation shadow price corrections to commodity prices, but not for the placing of too much stress upon the precise results derived therefrom. The main value of the exercise is the indication provided of the impact of a project on state income and the external trade position.

CHAPTER 5

COSTING THE FACTORS OF PRODUCTION

HAVING dealt with the valuation of commodities, both as inputs and outputs, we must now turn to the three classical factors of production – land, labour and capital – as inputs to a project. The problem is complicated by the fact that these are not commodities, as they relate to groups of people (landlords, workers and capitalists) who own the factors of production, and whose relationships determine the social system. Further, the payments made for these factors as inputs (rent, wages and profits) form the basis of the distribution of income in the economy. In the case of public investment projects the problem takes the specific form of valuing labour inputs on the one hand, and the external impact on rent and profits in the private sector on the other. State capital is another matter, and is treated separately in Part II of this book, where we discuss the allocation of public investment funds.

Here we shall first examine the valuation of land (and natural resources) in the context of its valuation for project appraisal, and then turn to the calculation of the 'shadow wage rate' used to cost the labour input, particularly that of unskilled workers. Finally we shall see why the profit element in input cost must be treated as income to owners of capital rather than a true input in its own right.

Land and Natural Resources

Under the general heading of 'land' we include not just land in its normal agricultural or urban-construction sense but also natural resources such as mineral deposits or fishing reserves. The approach to the valuation of all these is similar, none the less. In cases where the exploitation of the resource is the project

45

itself, there is no analytical problem, as the Net Present Value of the project is the economic value of that resource. Taking the case of, say, the appraisal of a project to exploit coal reserves for electric power generation, we would calculate the investment and operating costs of this and the alternative (stations powered by imported fuel oil), discounting both to the present. The difference between the two would be the value of the coal reserves to the economy. This value (shown as £500 million in the table below) will clearly depend crucially upon the expected price of oil and might (if this were low enough) be negative.

VALUATION OF COAL RESERVES (£m.)

Coal fuelled		Oil fuelled	
Investment cost	800	Investment cost	450
Operating costs	200	Operating costs	150
	1000	Imported oil	900
Differential	500		
Total	1500		1500

The valuation of land itself when it is the subject of a productive investment (as in an irrigation scheme) is carried out on the same principles, the difference between the Net Present Value of the value of output and its inputs being the economic valuation. An example was given, in fact, in Chapter 3. In general, for a stream of net income (x_t) accruing in each year (t), the present value (X) is given by applying the planning discount rate (r) over infinity:

$$X = \sum_{t=1}^{\infty} \frac{x_t}{(1+r)^t}$$

This is a finite sum because the net income will not have a growth rate as high as the discount rate over any long period. Given the value of this former (z) and the net income in the base year (x_0) and a steady rate of growth, then the present value can be expressed as:

$$X = \frac{x_0}{r-z}$$

In the case where the land has a net product in the base year of £50 per hectare, a historical trend in productivity of 2 per cent and there is a discount rate of 10 per cent, then the present value will be

$$X = \frac{£50}{0.10 - 0.02} = £625 \text{ per hectare}$$

The difficulty of forecasting over a long period is mitigated by the fact that by far the greater part (80 per cent in this example) is accounted for by the first twenty years.

In the case where the land or natural resource input is indirect (i.e. not owned by the project agency or controlled by the state), then the apparent 'cost' to the economy is in fact the rent paid to the owner of the resource. There may be a means of establishing an independent value for the product so obtained if it is a traded good, but if it is a product such as sand or gravel, or otherwise unsaleable timber, then the payment is just an income increment to the owner, and must be treated as such. It is, of course, equivalent to an external benefit of the type discussed in Chapter 3 in that case.

The valuation of land, as we have said, will depend upon the value of future income streams arising from the use of that land. In consequence, the valuation is not a given and objectively determinable amount (as would be, say, the cost of an imported machine) but rather the result of estimates of future production, the system of land tenure and uncertain factors such as international commodity prices in coming years. A planned programme for the introduction of high-yielding varieties will raise the future productivity and thus present value of agricultural land, while the expectation of relatively low world foodstuff prices in the future (or high fertiliser prices) would reduce it. More complex, but perhaps as important, is the fact that the subdivision, say, of a large coffee estate into peasant farms producing food crops might substantially change the income arising from the area, employment on the land and the distribution of wealth. Therefore the land will change in economic value according to the prevailing ownership institutions. However, once the tenurial and economic expectations have been defined, then the economic value can be established – in principle at least. The market will give a price based on similar considerations, but applied to the expectations of potential buyers and sellers, rather than those of the state and the economy as a whole. In cases where land is inalienable (e.g. ownership by kinship groups) the land may have no market price at all, while in other cases landlords may collude to offer low prices to an impoverished peasantry as they migrate to urban areas.

Urban land itself will, in a similar way, have a value related to its expected use. The difficulty here is that there is no physical output to be evaluated, and a coherent town planning system will allocate land uses according to an overall urbanisation programme largely independent of economic criteria; although cost considerations such as transport will clearly be relevant, social factors will presumably predominate. The market, in this case, will be even more unreliable as an indicator of economic value, particularly since the supply may be in the hands of relatively few speculators and demand is generally a function of the income levels of the existing or potential inhabitants of the zone. In consequence, reference to market valuation of land in establishing, say, the least-cost route for an urban expressway would tend to prejudice the poor as opposed to the rich citizen, as the market price of land of otherwise identical physical characteristics (e.g. the distance from the town centre) will be higher in the zone where the rich choose to live. Therefore urban land probably cannot be valued on a marginal basis for the purposes of cost–benefit analysis.

Natural resources are conventionally divided between those that are 'renewable' and others that are 'non-renewable'. Land itself is a typical case of the former, and petroleum of the latter, although the dividing line between the two is not a sharp one – land, for example, can be depleted by overcropping and erosion. Moreover, crucial living resources such as forests and fishing grounds are renewable (i.e. they reproduce themselves) only if the maximum offtake is not exceeded. None the less, these are classed as natural resources as opposed to 'man-made' crops because they exist naturally in exploitable quantities. The particular problem of valuing offtake from a non-renewable resource (such as a copper mine) is that more production now means less later, so that the opportunity cost can only be expressed in terms of income foregone in the future. In technical terms, this can be done by establishing an optimal depletion programme, maximising the net present value of income arising from different combinations of output over time subject to the overall reserve constraint, and then examining the effect upon the net present value of varying the offtake for the year in question, with compensating variations elsewhere in the depletion programme.

To illustrate this argument, we can take the simplest case of a resource to be exploited fully over two years – this assumption being merely to simplify the algebra. The offtake in each year (x_1, x_2) has been planned, and the present value (X) is given by discounting to the base year, given the prices* expected in those years (p_1, p_2):

$$X = p_1 x_1 + \frac{p_2 x_2}{1+r}$$

In the circumstance where the resource is renewable, then the economic value of expanding production in Year 1 is quite simply

$$\frac{dX}{dx_1} = p_1$$

But where it is non-renewable, then there is an additional relationship to express the limit of the reserves $(\bar{x})$, which in this case are all exploited:

$$x_1 + x_2 = \bar{x}$$

so we must write the present value equation as

$$X = p_1 x_1 + p_2 \frac{(\bar{x} - x_1)}{1+r}$$

and the value of expanding production in the base year is now

$$\frac{dX}{dx_1} = p_1 - \frac{p_2}{1+r}$$

which is less, of course, than the previous result, because the foregone (and discounted) income in the second year is deducted. Indeed if prices in Year 2 are higher than those in Year 1 by more than the rate of discount, then this value will be negative.

*Net of costs, in other words, the marginal economic value of the resource in that year.

The central analytical point is this: costing a resource input is not just a static phenomenon, but will involve judgements as to future developments.

Labour

Labour, being the only animate input to a project, is not only the fundamental one but also the objective of development planning in the widest sense: the provision of adequate employment and income opportunities for all members of the community. Human labour is not a commodity, and its 'price' (the wage rate) is also the means of sustaining a man and his family. This wage rate is determined by social and political considerations as much as by 'market forces' and, as importantly, the calculation of the opportunity cost of labour in economic terms must be distinguished from judgements as to the desirability of the wage rate actually paid. We are concerned, then, with the evaluation of the labour input to a project in the form of wages paid to those employed in its direct construction and operation, or in the economic activities involved in the estimation of external costs and benefits, or in the calculation of the shadow price of non-traded inputs. We shall take skilled and unskilled labour separately, because these are usually assumed to be in short and excess supply, respectively, and certainly require different criteria for valuation.

Starting with unskilled labour, this may be pragmatically defined as labour on jobs with no educational requirements or training of more than a few months' duration – in other words, jobs which a rural migrant might expect to fill. The problem arises* because there is an excess supply of unskilled labour for the available jobs in the 'modern' sector of the economy, where the wage is usually well above the income obtainable in alternative employment (agriculture or urban services), and certainly much greater than the alternative marginal productivity. In consequence, the cost to the economy of the transfer of labour is not the wage rate paid, but rather the much lower productivity in the sector from which the unskilled labour is drawn – typically peasant agriculture. This latter, then, forms the basis for the 'shadow wage rate' (SWR), which is usually expressed as a proportion of

*The problem of labour absorption and ' choice of technique ' is discussed more fully in Chapter 11.

the wage rate actually paid for unskilled labour employed on public sector projects. Although the SWR will vary according to the area from which the labour is drawn, the time of year and other factors we shall discuss below, it is current practice for the value to be worked out by the central planning office and then used on projects generally.

The marginal product in agriculture (m) from which unskilled labour is drawn is central to the calculation of the SWR, but involves a number of statistical problems and the adjustment of agricultural input and output values to reflect shadow prices. The scale of the research undertaken to establish the exact values will depend upon both the data sources available and the sensitivity of project decisions to the result. None the less, the concept is quite clear, and in practice the marginal productivity of labour in agriculture will be greater than zero and less than the average product – output in peasant agriculture divided by the work-force – due to declining return to labour. Thus it is now conventional* (given the relatively small magnitudes involved) to take an average of these two:

$$m = \tfrac{1}{2}a$$

For example, a major public construction project requires several thousand labourers paid a wage rate of 10 pesos a day, leading to a total wage bill for the project of p. 2.5 million in the total construction costs. The average annual product in peasant agriculture for the region (i.e. value added divided by the work-force) is roughly p. 1,000, equivalent to about p. 4 a day, so that

$$m = \tfrac{1}{2}.4 = 2$$

The shadow wage rate, if its definition is limited to the alternative product of labour, is then

$$\overline{W} = m = 2$$

and is expressed as a proportion of the market wage (W):

$$\frac{\overline{W}}{W} = \frac{m}{W} = \frac{2}{10} = 20\%$$

This ratio is then applied to the total wage bill of p. 2.5 million

*See, for example, Little and Mirrlees (1974), p. 277.

to give a 'shadow cost' or 'opportunity cost to the economy' of p. 0.5 million.

The elaboration of this approach (which gives a relatively low value for the SWR in general practice) has involved three important additions. The first stems from the fact that changing jobs normally means a change of location for the family, and thus the cost to both the family (e.g. new houses) and the state (e.g. new public utilities) may well have to be included in the shadow wage rate estimate. Any taxation paid by labour is also a net benefit to the state (social security payments must be balanced against disbursements, of course) and can thus be deducted from the cost of labour. The second arises from the fact that the process of migration leads to the existence of large slums or 'shanty towns' around metropolitan and regional cities, surplus labour which cannot be absorbed into regular employment.* The use of labour from this 'reserve' might well involve no loss in production whatsoever, as those engaged in small-scale urban service activities have little or no marginal product in terms of physical production and their contribution to services can easily be covered by others in the activity. The third emerges from the fact that the opportunity cost of labour in rural areas on public projects often reflects the seasonal nature of agricultural production. In other words, the use of local labour to build rural roads in the 'dry' aseason (when there is little need for labour inputs on the farms) might have no opportunity cost at all, while the same activity in the harvest or planting season might involve a very high opportunity cost in terms of the crops lost. In the numerical example of the previous paragraph, the estimate for the year as a whole might have to be divided into seasonal values in order to circumvent this difficulty.

Another approach to the determination of the opportunity cost of labour is through the rural wage rate. The argument is that agricultural enterprises employ labour up to the point where its marginal product equals the market wage for 'free' (e.g. landless) rural labour and thus this latter can be used as an estimate for m. Suppose that the current wage is 200 escudos a day in the harvest season (50 working days out of the 300) and there is rural unemployment the rest of the year with a going wage of only

*See Chapter 11.

75 escudos. For labour used on public works during the harvest, 200 escudos a day would be the shadow wage, out of season it would be 75, and for employment lasting the whole year the equivalent of 88 per day. The corresponding ratios, for a wage-rate on public works of 250 escudos *per diem*, are 80 per cent, 30 per cent and 35 per cent respectively.

Finally, the analysis of the market for unskilled labour (for that is what the estimate of *m* involves) should be extended in order to take into account the migratory process explicitly. To the extent that migration of surplus labour from the countryside towards unproductive service activities in the towns is already taking place, then the 'diversion' of labour from this stream will not involve any cost to the economy at all. Thus labour on *rural* public projects may well have an *m* of zero. Conversely, the expansion of urban employment in the state sector may well increase the migratory flow because of the extra urban income earning opportunity created by both the departure of the employee from the urban 'pool' and his greater expenditure on services. Thus labour on *urban* projects may have an *m* greater than the marginal product in agriculture. The correct solution therefore depends not on a general rule but upon empirically sound modelling of the relevant labour market.

These measures are 'static' in the sense that they examine the cost of labour to the economy in the short run. The basis of agricultural opportunity cost, even with the additional considerations, generally seems to lead to a SWR between a quarter and a half the market wage, which has important implications for the adoption of labour-intensive methods in project construction and operation. However, we should also consider the 'dynamic' implications of the additional employment in terms of the larger wage bill and thus a higher level of consumption in the economy. We shall take this up again in Part II, but here the main point is that some cost might well be attributed to the consumption increment arising from the shift from low to a higher wage income. For a given unit cost (v) and increase in consumption per worker (c), then the shadow wage rate would be redefined as

$$\overline{W} = m + v.c$$

The consumption increment (c) is, in fact, the wage paid less the loss in agricultural output (m) as long as the wage rate is fixed in real terms (W):

$$\overline{W} = m + (W - m)v$$

The difficulty then lies in the costing (v). The point is that where there is a shortage of savings in the economy (particularly in the public sector), then an expansion of consumption worsens this, so that at the extreme this increment would represent an absolute cost (i.e. $v=1$) so that the shadow wage is equal to the real wage $(\overline{W}=m+W-m=W)$. At the other extreme, when the savings–consumption balance is correct, and the two are equally valuable, then there is no cost $(v=0)$ and thus the SWR is once again the 'static' opportunity cost $(W=m)$. The value (v) can only be calculated by the central planning office in the light of macro-economic considerations. Taking, for example, a case where the planning office believes that an extra unit of savings is twice as valuable as a unit of consumption (i.e. $v=\frac{1}{2}$) would, with our previous values for the other parameters, yield

$$\overline{W} = 2 + \tfrac{1}{2}(10-2)$$
$$\frac{\overline{W}}{W} = \frac{6}{10} = 60\%$$

In general, then, this leads to higher values for the SWR, and in practice values seem to turn out between a half and three-quarters of the market wage. It should be noted that this point is distinct from any weight to be given to the income of wage earners as part of the analysis of income distribution, which we shall discuss in Chapter 6.

Turning now to skilled labour, the situation is somewhat different due to the fact that there is generally a deficit rather than a surplus in a developing economy, although this is not necessarily true in all branches, as the recent experience with university graduates in India and Sri Lanka has shown. In theory, the cost to the economy of using, say, a civil engineer on a public project is his potential contribution to productivity in another sector if he had not been so used – a cost that it is not possible to calculate in practice, in contrast to the case of unskilled labour we have just examined. The only way out, then, is to base the valuation on the salary being paid, adjusted for any taxation element. This is inevitably a compromise, but it implies that there is a reasonable degree of competitive bidding between employers (including the state) for their services and thus that the salary offered is commensurate with the skilled man's economic contribution. This difficulty is not as great as it might seem because the proportion of skilled salaries in the total labour bill is usually not very large. The allocation of skilled labour, moreover, is not usually planned on a project-by-project basis but rather by means of a national 'manpower plan'. This involves the estimation of future needs of each sector in terms of the skilled personnel required to conform with the planned expansion of the sector (e.g. agronomists for a particular rural region) and the structuring of the educational system (particularly technical training at the secondary and tertiary level) in line with these projected requirements. It is the success of methods such as these that lead to balanced allocation of skilled labour, rather than adjustment at a project level.

Finally, this would seem to be an appropriate point at which to discuss briefly two aspects of education apparently relevant to cost–benefit analysis. First, that an important aspect of a large project may well be the training for members of the work-force involved. For instance, a construction project might well produce skilled drivers and gang foremen, while a fisheries scheme might produce engine mechanics. In both cases, it would seem reasonable to assume that the cost of training is at least balanced by the benefit to the economy, and thus we could continue to cost these men at the SWR for unskilled labour. Second, that attempts have been made to assess the value of education as a whole (as opposed to specific vocational training) within a cost–benefit framework. The suggested method is based on the measurement of the lifetime income-streams of, say, a university graduate in a certain profession with those of a non-graduate. The difference (the 'benefits' of education) is then compared with the 'investment' element in the educational expenditure and the income foregone by attending university, producing an internal rate of return – supposedly the return on investment in 'human capital'. The major fallacy in this is one of direction of causation: educational attainment may not be the only or even the main determinant of higher income levels, particularly in the non-scientific subjects; on the contrary, social position (often inherited) determines the opportunity to gain both the education and the lucrative job subsequently.

Capital

The difficulty encountered by any theoretically or practically sound method of measuring 'capital' as an input to production lies at the centre of debates on the very principles of economics themselves. Indeed it forms the dividing line between the neo-classical 'economic scientists' and the radical 'political economists'. The point of difference is that while land and labour can be defined in 'physical' terms as distinct from ordinary commodities, and their payment (rent and wages) related to some real product, it is not really possible to do this for capital. Certainly assets (such as factories and roads) exist, and the owners of capital receive profits. However, we already have a method for valuing commodities, and these 'assets' are merely commodities purchased in the past, and probably containing an element of labour and land in their installation. In consequence, to what does the 'profit' payment correspond?

In practical terms, suppose that we were calculating the input cost of a non-traded good in the manner indicated, in Chapter 4, we would find that the 'capital good' (the transport equipment in the example) is costed already as a commodity input in the usual way, but that over and above this we have the profit margin accruing to the transport operator. This does not happen in the case of the labour input to the same project, as the wage (or shadow wage) item is the only entry. The explanation, of course, is that the capitalist, as the organiser of production, is in a position to extract income over and above the cost of the equipment he provides. To a certain extent this profit payment includes compensation for his own labour input, but strictly this should be included under the 'labour' item in the computation. As well, a certain proportion of the profit may be set aside for depreciation, but again this has been accounted for in the 'equipment' item as the portion of the machine's useful life 'spent' on the project. So the true profit element, once these adjustments have been made, is in fact net new income to the owners of capital, and not a cost at all: we are not measuring the use of some other input called 'capital'.

To summarise, gross profits may contain three elements: the labour payment to the capitalist as skilled organiser, the provision for reinvestment and net income increment to the owner of capital. These can be analysed in terms of shadow wage rates, commodity valuation and distributional criteria, respectively. We then find that the profit element in inputs to a public sector project are just external benefits of the type discussed in Chapter 3, while of course any profits accruing to the state through the project agency are state income like any other. There is no need, therefore, for a separate category 'capital' as an input. This is *not*, of course, equivalent to either asserting that there is no problem about the balance of savings and consumption in the economy (indeed, it is treated explicitly in Chapter 5 above) or that there is no need to ration state investment funds, which is the concern of Chapter 8.

Further Points

The evaluation of the three factors of production is still a matter of considerable dissent. This is not, however, a matter of developing a 'better technique' to resolve the difficulties. Rather, the problem arises from the fact that land, labour and capital are not commodities but involve ownership relationships which form the basis of the social system, the income arising from the three (rent, wages and profit) underpinning the structure of the personal income distribution. In consequence, attempts to measure, or even make precise statements about, the costs of factor inputs inevitably contain assumptions as to the present (or desired) nature of the socio-political system – in other words, an ideological element is unavoidable.

Occasionally it is suggested that foreign exchange should be treated as a separate 'factor' of production. This is a misconception, because foreign exchange only has a meaningful economic existence in terms of the commodities that can be purchased with it, and these are already handled by the methodology for traded goods explained in Chapter 4. It is certainly true that foreign exchange is particularly valuable in a double sense. First, that it allows one commodity (e.g. iron ore) to be transmuted into another (e.g. machine tools) through international trade rather than industrial processing, and second that it is generally 'scarce' in the sense that there is always a pressure of import expenditure against the constraint of export income. However, both of these are handled through the methodology just referred to, the latter by the explicit adjustment for the differential between domestic and international price levels. In practice, the inverse of the 'standard conversion factor' is sometimes known as the 'shadow exchange rate' (e.g. in the UNIDO method), but this refers to a ratio between two levels of commodity prices (domestic and international) and not to some new factor of production.

The best reading on the valuation of factor inputs is mostly contained within the standard texts on project appraisal, particularly OECD (1968) and UNIDO (1972). However, the problem of the shadow wage rate for unskilled labour in its various manifestations has received much wider attention because it expresses the nature of the 'labour-surplus' economy in an operative form. The seminal work in this field is Lewis (1954), but Galenson and Leibenstein (1955) introduce the 'consumption cost' and Little and Mirrlees (1974) draw together the strands for the composite formula we have discussed. An extremely detailed application of this formulation is contained in Seton (1972), while Todaro (1969) establishes the basis for the inclusion of migration and urban underemployment, both these being criticised and reformulated in FitzGerald (1976c). The methods of manpower planning and cost–benefit analysis of education are discussed in Blaug (1968). Finally, the debate over the nature of capital is ably summarised in Harcourt and Laing (1971).

CHAPTER 6

THE DISTRIBUTION OF COSTS AND BENEFITS

To the extent that it has become part of conventional wisdom that not just the growth in national income but also its distribution is an important element of the definition of 'development', it follows that the evaluation of the distribution of the Net Present Value of a project should be an important part of the project appraisal exercise. This distribution has various dimensions: that between one nation and another, between regions within a country, and between economic groups.

The analysis of the distributional impact of public investment is still a comparatively recent innovation although it is increasingly included in project reports, particularly the construction of the 'planning balance sheet'. The application of 'weights' so as to bias project choice in favour of those investments which involve income redistribution towards the poor and reduce the differentials has not, however, been as widely implemented in practice as it has been accepted in principle, for reasons that are discussed at the end of this chapter.

Income Weighting and Utility Theory

The expression of a policy to reduce income differentials should logically take the form of the setting of 'weights' (w_j) by which the net income increment (x_j) accruing to different groups (j) as a consequence of the project are multiplied, producing a measure of 'social value' $(\mathcal{Z})$ rather than the 'economic value' provided by the net present value (V). In algebraic terms, instead of

$$V = \sum_j x_j$$

we have

$$Z = \sum_j x_j w_j$$

The degree to which the subdivision into groups (j) is carried out depends upon the nature of the project. The 'normal' case where no weighting is applied is, in fact, an example of unitary weighting:

$$w_j = 1$$

$$Z = \sum_j 1.x_j = \sum_j x_j = V$$

The theoretical justification for such weighting is based on that aspect of welfare economics known as utility theory. The principle applied is that the value of an extra unit of income to a rich man is less than that to a poor man, an axiom that cannot be objectively proved, but seems to be a reasonable assumption. In formal terms, the marginal utility (u_j) to a certain person or group of extra income (x_j) is a function of their existing income (y_j):

$$u(x_j) = f(y_j)$$

of a form such that, the higher the latter, the lower the former:*

$$\frac{du}{dy} < 0$$

A widely used form of this relationship which has the required technical properties, is known as the 'Bernoulli form' having the characteristic of a constant 'elasticity' (a) less than zero:

$$w_j = u_j = A.y_j^a \qquad A, \text{ constant}$$

Although the subdivision of the costs and benefits of a project, discounted to the present, is not a difficult task, it can be extremely revealing. The setting of the weights is not, in contrast, an objective piece of analysis but depends upon a policy decision by the authorities, and should clearly derive from overall policy on

---

*Moreover, it is conventional to assume that the effect increases with income: $d^2u/dy^2 > 0$.

income distribution. For the purpose of argument, in the rest of this chapter we shall employ a particularly simple formulation,* with a 'unitary elasticity', where the weights are defined as the inverse ratio between the per capital income of the group in question (y_j) to the national average ($\bar{y}$):

$$w_j = \frac{\bar{y}}{y_j}$$

This is quite a powerful weighting system, implying that an extra pound to a man earning £1000 a year is worth five times as much as it is to a man earning £5000. An alternative approach to deriving the elasticity (a) from government policy, albeit indirectly, is to assume that marginal tax rates (both direct and indirect) are set by the government so as to be inversely related to the marginal utility of income to the taxpayer,† but this assumes a degree of rationality, independence and impartiality on the part of the state which may not obtain in practice.

Distribution and the Nation State

The most clear cut example of distributional weighting is in fact in conventional use: the distinction between costs and benefits accruing 'at home' and 'abroad'. Insofar as we regard, say, any net profit to the nation in international trade as a gain and not a transfer in national accounting, we are implying that the weight to be given to costs and benefits accruing to foreigners is zero. By 'foreign' in this context we would mean funds actually 'crossing the frontier', because foreign firms domiciled in the country in question count as domestic for the purpose of economic (as opposed to political) analysis.

Without anticipating the discussion at the end of this chapter, the next point to be considered is the extent to which income or

---

*This is the 'Bernoulli' form with the parameters set at: $A=\bar{y}, =-1$. This value is recommended by IBRD (1975), p. 103,

†If the *marginal* tax rate on the £5000 a year man is 70%, and on the £1000 a year man is 10%, then the implication is that the government believes that 10p in the extra pound for the poor is a burden equal to 70p for the rich. In other words, that an extra pound to the poorer man is worth seven times as much to him as to the richer of the two, and thus the respective weights should be in the ratio 7:1.

costs to the *state*, or 'public sector' can be considered as differing from income or costs to the 'private' sector. Although the former is not difficult to define, it is necessary to be more specific about the latter, as it makes a considerable difference whether we are talking about peasant farmers or industrial capitalists. None the less it would seem logical, although somewhat loose in terms of political philosophy, to regard the state as representing the economy as a whole, and thus *define* the appropriate weight as being unity: in other words, equivalent to that of the person or household with average per capita income. However, because the state can also operate as a centre of accumulation (generating savings and acting as a leader in the process of investment) while suffering from revenue constraints, extra income (or costs) to the state may be considerably more valuable, from the point of view of the central planner, than income to the 'average national' – a topic that we shall take up again in Part II. The important point here is that the valuation will depend upon the strategic role of the state in the process of accumulation.

Taking as an example a tourism project, we would have public investment in infrastructure (such as roads, airport extensions) and both domestic and foreign private investment in hotels, entertainment and other services. The layout of the 'planning balance sheet' is shown in the table, with the discounted investment costs and accumulated profits (apart from investment) separately indicated, and tax displayed as direct income to the state and a cost to the private sector. This layout should be contrasted with the traditional presentation in project reports, which would correspond to the extreme right-hand column. In consequence, although private investors benefit from the project to the extent of 130 million dinars, the net cost to the state and the profit outflow to foreign investors is such that there is an overall net *loss* to the economy of 30 million dinars. If we were to weight foreign benefits and costs at zero, and both state and private domestic flows at unity, then the NPV of the project is not positive, as it appeared at first sight, but negative.

TOURISM PROJECT (DINARS M. DISCOUNTED)

	Public	Domestic Private	Total	Foreign private	Overall total
Investment	210	150	360	100	460
Gross profits	..	250	250	260	510
Gross surplus	−210	+100	−110	+160	+ 50
Tax	+130	− 50	+ 80	− 80	..
Net surplus	− 80	+ 50	− 30	+ 80	+ 50

Another interesting illustration of this principle is the analysis of foreign finance for public investment. This usually involves, in the case of intergovernmental or multilateral-agency loans, concessionary terms* that can be evaluated in terms of the 'grant element' in such a loan, which arises because the loan disbursement is considered as a net benefit to the economy and the debt servicing as a net cost, but as the planning rate of discount (representing the opportunity cost of investment funds) is usually higher than the rate of interest on the loan, the value of the finance is greater than its cost. The technique for calculation consists in the entry of the foreign exchange transactions involved within a cash-flow framework – the initial disbursement and the repayment of principal and interest in stages after the grace period – and the application of the planning discount rate to find the present value. Thus a loan of $50 million with a three-year grace period, a five-year repayment period and a 5 per cent interest rate would have a debt schedule as shown in the table. The Net Present Value, after discounting at 12 per cent is the 'grant element': in this case equivalent to 41 per cent of the original loan value. Naturally, if this is a 'tied' loan involving the purchase of equipment from the lending country at prices above the international market, the differential should be deducted from the grant element.

*That is, interest rates or repayment timetables less costly than those offered by commercial banks. This may also involve political consequences which are not our concern here, but are mentioned in Chapter 11.

GRANT ELEMENT IN A LOAN ($m.)

Year	Loan flows	Discount factor	Discounted flows
0	+50.00	1.000	+50.00
1	—		—
2	—		—
3	—		—
4	−11.55	0.636	−7.35
5	−11.55	0.567	−6.55
6	−11.55	0.507	−5.86
7	−11.55	0.452	−5.22
8	−11.55	0.404	−4.67

| | Grant element: | | +20.35 |

Regional Distribution

An aspect of the 'distribution of development' that has come to be recognised as being of crucial importance is the disparities that emerge between regions within a nation, gaps which appear to grow over time in the majority of cases as production in the richer industrialising areas of a country (often around the principal cities) expands more rapidly than in the poorer rural areas. Although regional imbalance involves the concentration of markets and lack of integration between different productive sectors which may impede economic growth, there is also a major equity issue involved, and a development policy designed to reduce the disparity would logically imply weighting in project choice where allocation of public investment to different regions is involved.

The principle of regional weighting follows logically from the formula discussed above, and is possibly the aspect of weighting most easily accepted by government, although not necessarily implemented consistently. The NPV of the project is broken down to show a 'regional planning balance sheet' which gives the impact of costs and benefits upon different regions and the flows not attributable to any particular region, such as central government activities. The methodology is quite simple, and is best illustrated by an example, such as the planned allocation of investment to transport facilities in two regions – Oxonia and Cantabria. There are funds (up to ten million Grads) in the National Transport Plan for a new port, but there is some dispute over which region should 'get' the investment. A cost–benefit analysis is carried out, and the results are shown below, divided between the regions and the nation as a whole:

NPV(Grads m.)	If located in Cantabria			If located in Oxonia		
	Nation	Region	Total	Nation	Region	Total
Costs	9	1	10	7	2	9
Benefits	14	6	20	12	6	18
Surplus	5	5	10	5	4	9

It would seem that the project has a higher (unweighted)NPV if located in the Cantabria region, and thus we would initially choose that location for the port. It might well be, however, that Oxonia is considerably poorer than Cantabria, in which case there would exist an argument for locating it in Oxonia. Given the weighting formula:

$$w_i = \frac{\bar{y}}{y_i}$$

and the data:

	Income/head (Grads/annum)	Weight
Cantabria	800	0.75
Oxonia	400	1.50
Nation	600	1.00

then the *weighted* net benefit to each region can be compared, and a total figure derived – the *social benefit*. As can be seen, this analysis indicates that the project should, in fact, be located in Oxonia.

	If located in Cantabria		If located in Oxonia	
	Unweighted	Weighted	Unweighted	Weighted
Surplus to:				
Cantabria	5	3.8	—	—
Oxonia	—	—	4	6.0
Nation	5	5.0	5	5.0
	10	8.8	9	11.0

Distribution between Social Classes

Possibly the most contentious, and by the same token most important, aspect of distribution is that between different 'social' classes in the economy, such as capitalists, industrial workers, farmers, peasants and so on. Some economists would argue that this is not the proper concern of project appraisal, which should be concerned with 'efficiency', but others would argue that this is a key issue in 'development' and even that planning is meaningless without it. As we shall argue later on, both these views are somewhat mistaken, but the impact of public investment upon the incomes of different classes is clearly highly relevant to the development process. The appropriate weights to be applied should logically be consistent with the utility principle discussed above, but in doing so we throw into sharper relief the political implications of such application – in a way that national or regional weights do not – and thus there is generally less support for their use.

Even if we do apply them, however, there is an additional problem arising from the fact that private investment, and thus future incomes for all classes, is financed in part from capitalist profits, and therefore to the extent that these are reinvested they have a value distinct from the low weight we would attribute to them as the income of the rich. The exact value to be given will depend, however, upon the planned role of private investment in the economy – a point taken up in Part II.

We can extend the example of the irrigation project cited in Chapter 2 so as to lay out the distribution of costs and benefits perceived by the three groups concerned – the state, large farmers and small peasants – with production in the command area. Using the same procedure as before, we can also find the appropriate weights from the average income of large and small farmers, that for the state being unity by definition.

	Income/Household	Weight
	(p. '000 p.a.)	
Large farmers	50	1.3
Small farmers	20	3.3
National average	65	1.0

These are applied in the table below, which separates the costs and benefits to the farmers: the first figure in the top row being the discounted investment and maintenance costs and the third figure on the bottom row being the Net Present Value, as calculated in Chapter 2. The extra costs to the farmers would be new seeds and fertilisers needed for irrigated crops, plus extra labour and so on. Against this are set the gross extra benefits, as opposed to the net benefits used in Chapter 2. The multiplication of the third column by the weights in the fourth gives the fifth. The weighted social value is positive, as opposed to the negative unweighted value, because the farmers' income is below the national average.

PLANNING BALANCE AND SOCIAL VALUE: IRRIGATON PROJECT (PESOS M.)

	Costs	Benefits	Total	Weight	Social value
State	−20.3	..	−20.3	1.0	−20.3
Large farmers	−20.5	+35.0	+14.5	1.3	+18.9
Small farmers	− 1.4	+ 7.0	+ 5.6	3.3	+18.5
Total	−42.2	+42.0	− 0.2	..	+17.1

Two comments might be made on this planning balance sheet, which is not untypical for projects of this type. The first is that the bulk of the benefits are accruing to the large farmer (not 'estates' it is true, but households of an income approaching the national average) and not to the small, despite the fact that these latter make up the bulk of the households in the command area. The second, and this underlines a general theoretical difficulty in redistributive policy, is that it could be argued that the same distributional effect would be obtained from a straight gift of p. 20·1 million to the farmers, as opposed to the project under consideration which achieves the same effect at the greater cost of p. 20·3 million. Thus, in theory, 'efficient' decisions (i.e. on the basis of the unweighted Net Present Value) should be taken and then appropriate transfer payments made to meet distributive criteria – but this simplistic interpretation arises from a too narrow view of the problem of distribution. If a redistributive strategy is to have any real social meaning and permanence, it must not be seen as charity, but rather as a restructuring of the economy to the advantage of the poor. In this way, moreover, a potential for further autonomous growth in the area can be established.

Further Points

Before looking at some intrinsic problems arising from the introduction of distributive weights in project appraisal, and without anticipating the discussion of the setting of the public sector discount rate in Part II, the 'dynamic' implications of the method merit attention. When *per capita* national income is growing continuously over time, the marginal utility of these income increments will presumably fall, so that the value of future flows is less than that of present ones. If we apply the same weighting formula as before, then the ratio of weights in, say, Years 1 and 2 is the inverse ratio of income per head (y) in those years, and given the growth rate (s), then we have

$$\frac{w_1}{w_2} = \frac{y_2}{y_1} = \frac{y_1(1+s)}{y_1} = 1+s$$

In other words, the 'discount factor' that applies to income streams accrueing to persons is in fact the rate of growth of income per head. We do not use it as a planning discount rate as this must reflect the scarcity of investment funds, particularly to the state sector. However, if there were to be no shortage of funds and no alternative uses, then the planning rate would presumably approach the figure just derived.

The major problem with weighting would seem to be the question of who sets the 'alpha' parameter and how. Clearly this must reflect actual policy, and not the personal views of the project analyst, and thus requires a genuine government commitment to redistribution and a consistent determination to implement it, but the problem strikes much deeper because distributive policy cannot be separated from the whole 'style' of development. Income mal-distribution is closely connected to the system of production (i.e. choice of technique, pattern of output, regional balance), the form of ownership (e.g. land tenure), the structure of prices and the process of accumulation. It is not, therefore, an 'accidental' phenomenon separable from the rest of the economy, and it is closely related to the class structure as well, so that in consequence the objectives of, and constraints upon, state action in this field are a great extent endogenous rather than exogenous factors. This has two implications. First, that no real income redistribution can take place without a substantial change in the social and thus economic structure, and certainly not by marginal reorientation of public investments within the existing institutional framework. Second, to suggest that weighting should be applied to projects in the absence of such change is at best naïve and at worst a façade for continuing support of the *status quo*.

The literature on the topic of income distribution and development is voluminous and well known, but see Furtado (1970) for a pessimistic view, and Chenery (1974) for a more optimistic one. There is comparatively little written, however, on weighting systems. The concept of the planning balance sheet is well explained by Lichfield (1976), while both Little and Mirrlees (1974) and UNIDO (1972) explain the methodology of weighting itself, the latter proposing an ingenious but impracticable method of eliciting the key parameter from the minister concerned. McKean (1958) and Dorfman (1965) examine the implications for investment criteria in developed economies, but there is no equivalent study for less developed countries. However, Manne (1967) looks at the problem of regional weighting, Seton (1972) has an application to the shadow wage rate, Dobb (1970) discusses the application to the discounting of consumption in a socialist economy and Krutilla and Eckstein (1958) explain the 'marginal tax rate' method of eliciting weights from government policy in a developed capitalist economy. Finally, Stewart (1975) provides a caustic critique of the supposition that such weights can be applied without political change.

CHAPTER 7

FURTHER ASPECTS OF PROJECT
APPRAISAL

In a sense, the main strength and major weakness of project appraisal as a planning method lie in the extent to which it is separable from the national planning process as a whole. On the one hand, this separation allows for detailed adjustment to local circumstance, recognition of specific structural problems and plan implementation in a flexible, concrete and realistic manner – forming in effect the 'cutting edge' of effective planning. On the other hand, to the extent that it is separated from the national planning process, crucial aspects such as the valuation of non-traded output, the setting of the discount rate and the weight to be given to state income cannot be adequately handled.

The treatment of project appraisal as a separate topic, as is necessarily done in the 'manuals' has the additional difficulty that it takes the *status quo* (in terms of the structure of the economy, demand and supply in other branches, ownership patterns and so on) as given, and only considers marginal improvements in this structure. It is necessary, therefore, to see the planning process as a whole, which is why the exposition in this book is carried through to public investment programming as a whole. At this stage, however, we shall take up a number of points to conclude this first part, starting with a worked example to show how the various components of the cost–benefit analysis are brought together, followed by a discussion of the inclusion of measures of probability in the analysis, and concluding with a brief comparison of the methods of project appraisal in 'developed' socialist and capitalist economies.

An Illustrative Example

As we have considered the main elements of project appraisal separately, it might be useful to look at a numerical example that brings together the separate elements of the analysis. Rather than explain the derivation of each parameter value, a typical *layout* is given, the methodology for estimation being that given in the preceding chapters.

A small plant to produce fine silica from local sand deposits owned by a village cooperative is to be set up by the Rural Projects Division of the Ministry of Industry. The product will substitute for imported silica, and provide some employment for cooperative members outside the main agricultural seasons. However, there is an external disbenefit in terms of the land needed to build the plant and the hillside over which the washing channels (fed by spring water) will run. The social benefit of the project is probably considerable, as the community is a relatively poor one.

The known reserves of suitable sand will be enough for fifteen years' exploitation. In financial terms, there will be an investment cost of approximately one million dinars, from a loan provided by the National Development Bank on the recommendation of the RPD, and the estimated annual sales are 200,000 dinars against annual operating costs of 50,000 dinars. From this information we can work out the following present-value table in the usual way.

NET PRESENT VALUE OF PROJECT (DINARS '000 AT MARKET PRICES)

Sales of silica sand	10·38 ×	200	=	+	2076
Costs: Investment		1000	=	−	1000
Operations	10·38 ×	50	=	−	519
Net Present Value at 5% discount rate:				+	557

The Internal Rate of Return (the discount rate corresponding to a compounded discount factor over 15 years of $1000/150 = 6.67$) is 13 per cent. Thus the project is clearly viable in financial terms, and all the more so when it is remembered that for the cooperative as a whole the labour input to construction and operation is net new income, there being no other employment opportunities (short of migration) during the off-peak agricultural months, during which stocks of silica can be built up.

We now turn to the project from the point of view of the economy as a whole, represented by the planning office in the Ministry of Industry. The same basis of financial accounts is used, and appropriate shadow price 'adjustment factors' are applied to the components of the three main items (sales, operating and investment costs), the information being provided by the Ministry of Planning.

APPLICATION OF SHADOW PRICES

	Market value (D.'000)	Shadow/ market price (per cent)	Shadow value (D.'000)	Adjustment factor
Sales of sand	200	80	160	.80
Investment:				
Imported plant*	500	100	500	
Local materials	200	70	140	
Local labour	300	30	90	
	1000		730	.73
Operations:				
Labour	20	30	6	
Fuel	5	50	3	
Spares, sacks	10	90	9	
Transport	15	72	11	
	50		29	.58

The application is then quite simple, but involves the application of the higher 'planning' discount rate (12 per cent) as well:

ADJUSTMENT TO SHADOW VALUES

	Market prices (D.'000 at 5% discount rate)	Market prices (D.'000 at 12% discount rate)	Adjustment factor	Shadow prices (D.'000)
Sales of sand	2076	1362	.80	1090
Costs: Investment	1000	1000	.73	730
Operations	519	341	.58	198
Net Present Value	+ 557	+ 21		+ 162

*This includes the cost of engineering services.

The conclusion, then, is that the project has slightly less value to the economy as a whole than to the community in question. Most of the discrepancy arises from the fact that the National Development Bank will be lending at well below the opportunity cost of capital to the state (the planning discount rate), and this is only partly balanced by the other shadow price adjustments, which tend to favour the project. In addition, we now have to deduct the value of the land lost. This will be a much lower cost to the economy than to the cooperative, because of the different rates of discount used, even though the annual net economic value of the alternative product of that land is the same to both parties: 15,000 dinars a year.

EXTERNAL COST OF PROJECT

	Annual income (D.'000)	Discount factor	Present value (D.'000)
Market prices (5%)	15	10.38	156
Shadow prices (12%)	15	6.81	102

This means that we now have a reduced NPV and an almost marginal project in economic terms, although it is still well worthwhile from the point of view of the community. The overall totals, as conventionally set out, are in the next table.

SUMMARY OF PROJECT APPRAISAL

	Market prices		Shadow prices	
Direct benefits		2076		1090
Direct costs:				
Investment	1000		730	
Operations	519		198	
		1519		928
		557		162
Secondary costs		156		102
Net Present Value		+ 401		+ 60

The final step is to introduce distributive considerations, to allow for the fact that this community has an average income of about half the national average. If we use the simple 'unitary elasticity' formula for weighting of the type discussed in Chapter 6, this would mean that the cooperative should be given a weight of *two* as opposed to a weight of *one* for the rest of the economy and the state. The first task is to set out the 'planning balance sheet', which in this case is quite simple, because we already know the total costs and benefits to the cooperative on the one hand, and those to the economy as a whole on the other, so that the costs and benefits to the 'rest of the economy' must be the difference between the two. The result is shown below: the 'rest of the economy' item absorbs all the adjustments implicit in the conversion from market prices to shadow prices (as the first column is expressed entirely in terms of the former and the third in terms of the latter) to give the impact on the Net Present Value received elsewhere in the economy.*

INCOME WEIGHTING THE COST–BENEFIT ANALYSIS

(D.'000)	Cooperative	Rest of economy	Economy as a whole
Total project benefits	+2076		+1090
Total project costs	−1675		−1030
Net Present Value	+ 401	− 341	+ 60
Income weight	2·0	1·0	...
Weighted value	+ 802	− 341	+ 461

As can be seen, this exercise, the social value of the project redeems it from the marginal fate that it would suffer in purely economic terms, and specifies the real income transfer (0.34 million dinars) involved.

Multiple-purpose Projects

Multi-purpose projects give rise to the problem of joint costs, where the same project provides different economic outputs. An example would be a barrage with a road on top and hydroelectric facilities below. Some of the costs (e.g. maintenance of the hydro-

---

*In other words, it is the difference between the first column (i.e. the 'financial' analysis at market prices) and the third column (i.e. the 'economic' analysis at shadow prices) *by definition*.

plant) are separable, but a large part of the capital cost is joint to the three activities (irrigation, transport and energy) and attempts to separate it by function are in fact economically mis-conceived: if the cost is truly joint, then on grounds of economic efficiency the project must be considered as a whole. Multi-purpose projects are worth building if the *sum* of benefits from each purpose (net of separable costs) exceeds the joint-cost item. These projects will contain 'jointness' through time, of course, as well as that arising from the variety of services provided. It is important, none the less, to examine all possible combinations of the activities to find an optimum solution.

Let us examine a proposal to build a barrage (A) with a road (B) and a hydroelectric plant (C) as a joint project. As well as the full joint project $(A+B+C)$, we could omit the hydro-plant leaving $(A+B)$, or omit the road leaving $(A+C)$, or build the barrage alone (A). We could, moreover, build the road alone (B) by constructing a bridge, but we could not have the hydro-plant alone. The alternatives are shown in the table below, showing the costs and benefits of each project combination.

Project alternative	Costs	Benefits	NPV
$A+B+C$	70	90	+20
$A+B$	50	80	+30
$A+C$	60	70	+10
A	40	60	+20
B	30	20	−10

From this analysis we can see that:

(1) the multi-purpose project $(A+B+C)$ has a positive NPV $(+20)$ and thus it seems suitable for acceptance;

(2) if we remove the hydro-plant, however, leaving $(A+B)$, the NPV *increases* to $+30$, this change reduces costs by 20 and benefits by only 10, and is thus an improvement;

(3) to build the road (B) *alone* involves a bridge and in fact would give a negative NPV (-10) but when added to the barrage $(A+B)$ increases benefits by 20 while increasing costs by 10;

(4) the best solution, therefore, is to build the barrage and road only $(A+B)$, even though the entire multipurpose project

$(A+B+C)$ has a positive NPV.

This is a simple example, but illustrates the need to examine *project alternatives* with great care.

The Analysis of Uncertainty

An aspect of project appraisal that causes much concern is the problem of uncertainty about the future. This applies particularly to forecasts of the volume of demand and of the prices of commodities on international markets. To a certain extent this is alleviated by the planning system, which indicates the expected pattern of future events in a coherent manner, but exogenous factors, such as rainfall or export prices, are still subject to risk and uncertainty, and it would be realistic to allow for this within the development plan itself.

The formal difference between *risk* and *uncertainty* is that risk refers to cases where the nature of the probability distribution of future events is statistically known (e.g. life insurance tables), while uncertainty refers to cases where the probabilities are only guessed, although on the basis of available information (e.g. bets on horse-races).

In a project analysis, the Net Present Value $(\mathcal{Z})$ may depend upon one crucial variable, such as rainfall, (x):

$$\mathcal{Z}=f(x)$$

but the rainfall may be distributed in a certain probability distribution, in which case we should work with the *expected value* of the outcome:

$$E[\mathcal{Z}] = E[f(x)]$$

Moreover, if the variable is normally distributed with a known* standard deviation (σ), then the expected value can be related to the mean value of the variable (x), by Taylorian expansion:

$$E[\mathcal{Z}] \simeq f(\bar{x}) + \frac{\sigma^2}{2}f''(\bar{x})$$

It would also be advisable to examine a simpler method as well. A very popular way of handling uncertainty about the future is by estimating a 'high', 'best' and 'low' forecast of the relevant

*See any elementary textbook on statistics, such as Yeomans (1968).

variable (X_h, X_b, X_l) in which case the expected NPV can be estimated as:

$$E[Z] = \tfrac{1}{4}\left\{f(X_h) + 2f(X_b) + f(X_l)\right\}$$

This is a *triangular* distribution, which makes some allowance for asymmetry in the probability distribution. The 'high' and 'low' forecasts should be set so as to cover 95 per cent of the expected range of x-values.*

A specific example of such probability analysis is provided by flood control. The hydraulic engineers can assign specific probabilities to certain levels of rainfall, which in turn depend upon weather conditions, of which there are past records. To each rainfall level a probability level can be attributed,† and for each rainfall level there is a corresponding economic value (in terms of crop output, for instance) which will vary from zero in a drought, through a maximum, down to zero again under full flood conditions. We can thus construct a table of the following form:

Rainfall (cm)	Probability (per cent)	Benefit ($ '000)
10	10	0
30	20	80
50	40	120
70	20	60
100	10	0

and the expected value of the Benefits are thus given by:

$$10\% \times \quad 0 = \quad 0$$
$$20\% \times \ 80 = 16$$
$$40\% \times 120 = 48$$
$$20\% \times \ 60 = 12$$
$$10\% \times \quad 0 = \underline{\quad 0}$$
$$76$$

*For a normal distribution, the 95 per cent confidence intervals will be separated by approximately 4 standard deviations (σ). This parameter can also be estimated from the regression equation used to find the trend in the past of any variable – so long as this variance can be assumed to obtain in the future – as we saw in Chapter 1.

†These are, in practice, defined in terms of the 'return period' of a certain rainfall level. A ' return period of 20 years' is equivalent to a 5 per cent risk in any one year.

The expected Benefit is thus $76,000, which is quite different from the Benefit corresponding to the expected mean rainfall of 51 cm!

In an analysis of uncertainty, however, we will generally have much less information about the future, and it will usually be based on the 'best guesses' of the analysts concerned. A good example of this is export price forecasting in primary commodities. Supposing we are considering a plant for the production of palm oil for export, where market conditions are unstable. Our price forecast could be translated into revenue figures and discounted, to be compared with costs, as shown below:

	Discounted Revenues	Discounted Costs	NPV
Forecast:			
High	90	70	+20
Best	80	70	+10
Low	60	70	−10

The expected NPV would be calculated in this case by the 'triangular distribution' formula:

$$E[Z] = \tfrac{1}{4}(20+2.10-10)$$
$$= 7 \cdot 5$$

Thus there is an expected NPV of £7500. It should also be noted that there is a 25 per cent chance of the project failing altogether, and this may be unacceptable to the authorities.

Project Appraisal in Advanced Economies

Before concluding this part of the book, it would seem appropriate to digress slightly in order to discuss the way in which public investment is analysed in advanced economies, particularly because this contrast throws some light upon the approaches adopted in developing economies. If we can define, very broadly, the three key aspects of project appraisal as being the use of shadow prices, the analysis of externalities and the integration with the national planning system, then we can make the following general statement: in neither advanced capitalist nor socialist economies is shadow pricing applied to any great extent, but while in the socialist economies the link with national planning as a whole is strong and externalities generally ignored, the situation in capitalist economies is the reverse, with no central planning but extensive analysis of external effects.

Taking the socialist economies first, we find that project appraisal is conceived within a central planning framework, and this is its distinguishing feature. Analysis of individual projects in any but an engineering sense is a comparatively recent development, and is generally confined to the selection of a minimum-cost production solution among alternatives available so as to comply with supply requirements set by the central planners. The search for a minimum-cost solution across a broad range of alternatives means that the investment project results in a saving of current expenditure, which are the 'benefits' of the project. As far as is known, shadow prices for surplus labour, externalities and distribution weights are not applied, presumably on the grounds that these are handled directly through the broad structural reforms contained in the transition to socialism and subsequent economic strategy. Any methodology of project appraisal requires some means of relating future benefits to present investment costs, and until about a decade ago this was done by applying a 'pay back period' criterion. This measures the number of years taken for the accumulated benefits to equal to the investment costs, and the project variant with the lowest pay-back period is chosen; alternatively a 'cut-off' period can be set for screening projects for a particular sector, all those with a higher pay-back period being rejected. In fact, this is a very crude equivalent to the discount rate* with the disadvantage that it does not take into account costs and benefits beyond the pay-back period. In consequence, despite some opposition based on a dogmatic resistance to the idea of 'interest' as a capitalist concept, the use of the discount rate as a method of allocating investment funds has been introduced over the last decade, but with the title of 'index of investment efficiency'. Over the same period, some progress

*With equal annual income streams (x) accumulating over a pay-back period (N) to balance the capital cost (K), this is equivalent to a discount rate (R) such that:

$$\sum_{t=0}^{N} \frac{1}{(1+R)^t} = \frac{K}{x}$$

in the evaluation of 'foreign trade' projects (i.e. those concerned with exports or non-strategic imports) in terms of international prices rather than centrally set requirements has been made, which recognises the relevance, albeit on a limited scale, of the principles explained in Chapter 4. Also, on a broader scale, the gradual introduction of greater autonomy in decision making at plant level in industry has made project appraisal more relevant, although within an environment where the prices and total marketed volumes of inputs and outputs are still rigidly controlled.

Turning next to the advanced capitalist economies, the distinguishing feature is that in the absence of comprehensive planning public sector involvement with the economy is mainly confined to welfare services and physical infrastructure, so that it is the measurement of externalities that is furthest advanced – particularly in the United States and the United Kingdom. The most prominent projects, in relation to both absolute size and methodological advance, have been in transport investments such as roads and airports. It is generally assumed that market prices, where markets exist, are a reasonable indicator of value and that the existing income distribution is socially acceptable, so that the direct costs and benefits of a transport project can be handled in a 'financial' way. The focus of interest, therefore, is on the secondary costs and benefits which, in the case of transport projects, mean time savings to users of the facility on the one hand and environmental destruction on the other. The value of time saved to, say, urban commuters by the provision of an underground railway ('metro') is the principal benefit of such a project, and although the total quantity of time saved can be estimated from the mathematical models used to forecast the traffic flows, its valuation is not so clear. The traditional approach has been to take the average income level of the traveller* on the grounds that time lost is income lost. This is now considered to be unsatisfactory, as travel is often in 'own' time which is unavailable for work, or just for pleasure, and analysis of situations where travellers can choose between saving time or saving money (e.g. bus versus rail) does seem to show that people do in fact value their own time at about half their income level; this is now applied

---

*That is, an hourly rate equivalent to the annual income – roughly annual income divided by 2000.

widely in evaluating projects of this type. The costing of environmental impact is a topic of growing concern in advanced capitalist economies, which have successfully destroyed much of their own natural beauty. So far, the best (or rather, the only) method of doing this is to establish what the market is willing to pay for the 'amenity' provided by the environment. This can be done either by analysing land values in the area, to establish the premium paid for (say) proximity to a park, or ascertaining how much people are prepared to pay in order to visit a particular historical monument, in terms of entrance fees or travel cost to get there. These methods are open to obvious objections, particularly because, as the market in the past has destroyed the environment, it is difficult to see how it can be used to value future damage to it. It may well be that this sort of problem can only be dealt with in administrative terms, and is not susceptible to quantitative analysis.

It may reasonably be concluded from this short discussion of cost–benefit analysis in developed economies that the preoccupations of their planners are different from those in the developing economies. In particular, this reflects the fact that in capitalist economies the direct role of the state in production is much less, and in socialist ones much more, than in a typical developing economy. Moreover, in developed economies, by definition, the question of rapid structural change in the economy is not of such great importance. There is a grave danger, therefore, implicit in the direct transfer of analytical or planning techniques from developed to underdeveloped economies. Just two examples will illustrate this point. First, the 'developed socialist' methods of cost-minimisation *presuppose* an all-embracing central planning system, so that attempt to use them in cases where the state does not control the means of production have little meaning. Second, the method of valuing time in an advanced capitalist economy depends upon full employment and an acceptable income distribution, in the absence of which these methods would be severely misleading. Specifically, the first case might lead to the choice of capital-intensive projects as the low opportunity cost of labour would not be taken into account, while the second would lead to transport projects designed to ease the urban transit problems of the rich being given priority over rural penetration roads.

None the less, a grasp of the analytical principles underlying these methods, and of the debates surrounding them, can provide a valuable background to an understanding of the somewhat different problems of project appraisal in developing economies.

Final Points

This concludes the survey of project appraisal as such, but a number of the most important 'loose ends' are taken up in the second part of the book. In particular, the problems of relating projects to wider investment programmes, the analysis of linkages to other branches, the planning of non-traded output and the allocation of investment funds through the discount rate will be treated explicitly in the context of the planning of the public sector.

Reading material for the topics discussed in this last chapter is quite abundant, but little of it is directly applicable to project appraisal in developing countries. On probability analysis, however, both Poliquen (1970) and Reutlinger (1970) are very useful. Dasgupta and Pearce (1972) provide a good summary of cost–benefit in developed capitalist economies, and while Radowski (1966) explains the use of the 'investment efficiency' criterion in socialist countries in some depth, the more recent developments in Soviet planning are discussed in Ellman (1971), and those in Hungarian industrial programming by Kornai (1975). Mishra and Beyer (1976) is an excellent demonstration of how project appraisal methods should be applied in a practical case of fisheries development, and might well serve as a model for project presentation, particularly since very few of these reports are ever published. Finally, Scott *et al.* (1975) has a number of interesting illustrations of the way in which the Little–Mirrlees method has been applied in practice, and Roemer and Stern (1976) show how shadow prices might be calculated and applied within the context of a specific economy.

EXERCISES IN PROJECT APPRAISAL

In this section we present some exercises which can be worked through in order to gain a better understanding of project appraisal technique. They are mainly concerned with the mechanics of the analysis, though wider questions are raised for further discussion.

The first and second problems are simple exercises in discounting; the approach can be quickly revised by reference to Chapter 2. The third problem (a fishmeal plant) is more complex, and step-by-step guidance is provided so that the argument can be understood properly. The fourth and fifth problems are quite straightforward but of some interest in their implications. The last problem (irrigation) is the most difficult, and the data has been provided in a form that approximates to actual experience more than the previous ones. If possible, it should be carried out jointly by a small group: there is more than one possible 'solution' to this problem, and extra assumptions may be necessary during analysis.

(1) *Discounting Exercise*

A project has the following characteristics:

Investment cost:	£6000
Annual operating cost:	£ 500
Annual sales revenue:	£1500
Project life:	10 years

Calculate the Net Present Value at 5 per cent and 15 per cent discount rates. Then calculate approximately (to the nearest per cent) the Internal Rate of Return using a graph.

Investment cost	Operating cost	Total costs	Sales revenue	Net cash flow	5%		15%	
					Discount factor	Discounted cash flow	Discount factor	Discounted cash flow

NPV=

(2) *A River Port*

A project for the improvement of a fluvial port by the installation of new facilities will, it is calculated, cost some $1.5 million to build (in one year) and have an economic life of 20 years. The benefits will be a 25 per cent reduction in ship maintenance costs: these currently run at roughly $4000 a year for each of the 200 vessels using the port, which until the new quay is built are subject to considerable damage while unloading. Foreign finance is available at 10 per cent. Is the project economically feasible?

Set out your calculations in the table below, and give your conclusion.

Year	Costs	Benefits	Net flow	Discount factor	Discounted flow
0					
1					
2					
3					
4					
5					
6					
7					
8					
9					
10					
11					
12					
13					
14					
15					
16					
17					
18					
19					
20					

Net Present Value:

(3) *A Fishmeal Project*

Introduction

It is proposed to construct an anchovy processing plant in order to obtain fishmeal for export from previously unexploited areas off the coast of Wolfsonia. There are three aspects of the project that are important: the direct (financial) operation of the factory, the supporting infrastructure (roads etc.) and the impact on the present fishing operations.

We must carry out a cost–benefit analysis of all these aspects, following the steps indicated below, as an aid to decision making by the government, in order to establish:

(*a*) if the project as a whole is acceptable;

(*b*) if the factory is commercially profitable, and
  if not, what should be done;

and then go on to discuss problems such as location and ownership of the plant.

Project Data

The factory: Economic life is 10 years

Construction period: One year, ready at beginning of year 1

Processing capacity: 10,000 tons/year of fish required to produce 5000 tons/year of fishmeal exports

Employment: 100 men at 7000 dinars a year for operations

Construction cost: 10 million dinars, of which: imported equipment (including duty at 50 per cent) is 6m., unskilled labour 2m., and 'other inputs' 2m.

Operating costs: Some 50,000 dinars of imported goods and 25,0000 dinars of local materials are required, apart from the labour mentioned above, and the fish itself, at 100 dinars/ton.

Rate of interest
on bank loans: 8 per cent

First, fill in this table from the data provided:

FINANCIAL COSTS ('000 DINARS)

	Construction	Operation
Imports		
Unskilled labour		
Other inputs		
	————	————
	————	
Fish		————

The project requires some extra infrastructure, particularly the provision of a road (1·5 million dinars) and some improvements to the port facilities (0·5 million dinars). It is estimated that these costs will both be composed of 50 per cent labour and 50 per cent local materials.
Fill in the table below:

	Road	Port	Total
Unskilled labour			
Local materials			
	————	————	————
	————	————	————

In order to service the plant, the fishing cooperative must buy 20 new fishing boats, at a cost of 100,000 dinars each (tax-free).

The price (delivered at the factory) for anchovies is 100 dinars/ton, while their costs are some 10,000 dinars per ship per year for labour and 5000 dinars per ship per year for materials.

The state bank is financing the purchase of the craft with an IBRD loan, and calculates that the equivalent annual capital charge (i.e. amortisation) over their life to be one-tenth of the original sum.

	Dinars/ship/year	Dinars/ton	Dinars/year
Craft			
Labour			
Materials			
	_____	_____	_____
	_____	_____	_____

Price/ton

_____

=Profit/ton

_____

Export prices are presently at 500 dinars/tons for fishmeal exports, but are expected to rise to 600 dinars in Year 5 and remain there until Year 10.

Calculations

The first step is to undertake a financial analysis of the factory itself, in order to determine its commercial feasibility.

Fill in the table below, and calculate the Net Present Value with the 'rate of interest on bank loans'.

Year	Costs		Sales	Cash	Discount	Discounted
	Construction	Operations	revenue	flow	factor	cash flow
0						
1						
2						
3						
4						
5						
6						
7						
8						
9						
10						

NPV =

The economic analysis is a little more complex, and we have to do three things:

(a) adjust the factory study to economic costs;
(b) add in the infrastructure cost;
(c) add in the benefits to the fishing industry.

The main adjustments to economic costs are:

(i) elimination of the 50 per cent import duty for the factory plant;
(ii) the shadow price of labour is judged to be half its market cost.

First we must fill in the table below, comparing costs in market and shadow prices. The value of the output (exports) remains the same in both cases.

		Market prices	Shadow prices
Construction:			
Factory:	Imports		
	Labour		
	Materials		
Road etc.	Labour		
	Materials		
TOTAL CONSTRUCTION			
Operations:			
Factory:	Imports		
	Labour		
	Other Materials		
Fishing:	Labour		
	Materials		
	Craft		
TOTAL OPERATIONS			

We can now work out the NPV of the project as a whole, including all three aspects, discounting at 10 per cent, which is the planning discount rate in this case.

| Year | Costs | | Benefits | Net flow | Discount | Discounted |
	Construction	Operations	(exports)		factor	flow
0						
1						
2						
3						
4						
5						
6						
7						
8						
9						
10						

Net Present Value =

Having carried out the calculations above, we are now in the position to answer several specific questions:

(a) Is the factory feasible as a *financial* enterprise?

(b) Is the project as a whole a good thing from the economic point of view?

(c) What would happen if import duty was lifted for the factory?

(d) What if the price fell to 400 dinars/ton instead of rising in Year 5?

(e) What is the financial Internal Rate of Return for the factory?

(f) What is the IRR for the project as a whole?

For general discussion, the following points may also be considered:

(g) Should the project be in the public or private sector? State your reasons.

(h) If the fishmeal were sold locally for cattle-feed rather than exported, how would you establish its value?

(i) What elements should enter into a consideration of the best location for the project?

(j) What social and administrative issues do you think would be important in this case?

(4) *Choice of Cropping Patterns*

Table 1 shows the financial (i.e. market-price) costs and revenues involved in wheat and oilseed production. Fill in Table 2, taking into account the fact that the government is selling fertiliser at one-third below the market (i.e. import) price from the point of view of the farmer. Then fill in Table 3 from the point of view of the economy (i.e. the government), taking into account the fact that the opportunity cost (accounting price) of labour is half its market wage. Both wheat and oilseed are imported at the moment, at the international price.

TABLE 1
MARKET PRICE

		Wheat	Oilseed
Pesos/acre	Labour	80	60
	Fertiliser	60	45
Price/ton	Local (pesos)	100	60
	International($)	8	6
Yield: tons/acre		2.0	2.5
Exchange rate: $1 = 10 pesos			

TABLE 2
FARMER

		Wheat	Oilseed
Pesos/acre			
	Costs: Labour		
	Fertiliser		
	Total		
	Revenue		
	Gross Profit		

TABLE 3
ECONOMY

		Wheat	Oilseed
Pesos/acre			
	Costs: Labour		
	Fertiliser		
	Total		
	Revenue		
	Gross Benefit		

Answer the following questions:
- (a) Which crop will the farmer probably produce?
- (b) Which crop is economically best to grow?
- (c) What might the government do to change the position? Discuss alternative pricing policies in the light of both efficiency and distributive considerations.

(5) *Alternative Construction Methods*

There are two alternative methods for the construction of a major infrastructure project. The project variants are: (*A*) a capital-intensive method and (*B*) a labour-intensive method. The cost structure of the two variants is shown below.

Using this information, fill in the table on opportunity costs by computing the shadow prices and entering the results in the table provided.

INVESTMENT COSTS

(Financial Costs – $'000)

		A	B
Labour:	skilled	1,000	500
	unskilled	2,000	6,000
Materials:	local	500	3,000
	imported	1,500	1,000
Imported equipment		5,000	1,000
		10,000	11,500
Design and supervision		1,000	1,000
TOTAL		11,000	12,500

Unskilled labour will receive a wage of $100 a month on the construction of the project, but would otherwise work in agriculture earning $50 month, which is believed to approximate their marginal product in that sector.

Local materials are mostly quarried in the area, and its shadow price is estimated to be 60 per cent of the market price. Imported materials bear no duty.

Imported equipment does bear duty, of 25 per cent upon the c.i.f. price. You may make any other assumptions you think are necessary, but these must be clearly stated.

INVESTMENT COSTS

(Economic Costs – $'000)

		A	B
Labour:	skilled		
	unskilled		
Materials:	local		
	imported		
Imported equipment			
Design and supervision			
TOTAL			

(a) Which project variant would you recommend: on financial grounds? on economic grounds?

(b) What is the main reason for the difference between the financial and economic costs in this case?

(c) Discuss any other considerations (such as quality, speed of construction and budgetary impact) that might be relevant.

(6) *An Irrigation Project*
The Project

An irrigation scheme is proposed for the area known as Hauriendum, in the Western Province of Nusquam, through which flows the River Flumen. The total cost of the complete scheme (including all stages) will be some 24 million Soldi (s.), and would irrigate an area of about 5000 hectares.

The Economic Sub-committee of the Cabinet requires a short report on the project, including a cost–benefit analysis based upon the information given by:

(a) Pontifex and Partners – Consulting Engineers
(b) Cibus Research S.A. – Consulting Agronomists
(c) Chief Economist, Research Division, Ministry of Agriculture and Rural Development.
(d) Director, Planning and Budgeting Division, Ministry of Public Works.
(e) Director, Programming Section, National Planning commission.

The project should be examined from the point of view of both the local peasant population and the economy as a whole, and some consideration given to the possibility of pricing the water supply.

A short report should be prepared for discussion at the next meeting of the sub-committee.

The Analysis

The approach is your own group decision, but in broad terms it is necessary to establish at least the following:

(a) The Net Present Cost of the two construction schemes (1 or 1+2), both in economic and financial terms.
(b) The economic and financial benefits (present value) of the alternative cropping patterns (*A* or *B*) over the existing one, and the Net Present Value per hectare and for the two areas (1, 2) as a whole.
(c) Whether Scheme 1 or Schemes 1 *and* 2 should be chosen, on the basis of a cost–benefit analysis.
(d) The water charge needed to cover project outlays.
(e) The value of this project in relation to the others mentioned by the Ministry of Public Works.

Appendices

(a) *Engineering Cost Estimates*
(Pontifex and Partners, Consulting Engineers, Rome)

The River Flumen presently runs through Hauriendum in a deep 'canyon' formation, and is not used for irrigation purposes. The construction of headworks where the river enters the area (a valley floor) would allow a considerable area to be served by gravity irrigation. The basic design (Stage I) would include the headworks and an area of 3500 hectares, at a total cost of some S. 15 million. The system can be extended (Stage II) to cover an additional 1500 hectares by the construction of further canals and slight modification to the headworks. Stage II would cost some S. 3 million.

The construction schedule is such that expenditure would be spread over three years and exploitation could start in Year 4; the estimated project life being 40 years.

CONSTRUCTION OUTLAYS (S.m.)

	Year 1	Year 2	Year 3	Total
Stage I	3	9	3	15
Stage II			3	3

The operating costs are low, as they only involve maintenance with the use of local labour.

ANNUAL MAINTENANCE

Stage I	S. 300,000
Stage II	S. 50,000

At the request of the Planning Commission we have prepared estimates of the breakdown of the expenditure, based upon our experience in Nusquam.

	Construction (per cent)	Maintenance (per cent)
Imported equipment	20	—
Local materials	30	30
Labour: Skilled	10	15
Unskilled	30	50
	90	95
Design and supervision	10	5
TOTAL	100	100

(b) *Agronomic Estimates*
        (Cibus Research, Athens)

There are two alternative cropping patterns that would be suitable for the Hauriendum area, which is of even soil quality throughout. As at present, one crop could be grown, although the yields would, of course be much higher with irrigation.

The input requirements and eventual output level for these alternative patterns are shown below:

ALTERNATIVE CROPPING PATTERNS

		Present	A	B
Output (quintals/ha):	Maize	10	—	—
	Wheat	—	20	—
	Oilseed	—	—	12
Fertiliser (kg/ha)		—	100	240
Labour (man-days/ha):				
	Family	50	50	50
	Hired	—	25	20

It will take some time, probably three seasons, in order to achieve a complete conversion from the present cropping pattern to whichever (A or B) is chosen, especially since new cultivation techniques are necessary and the peasants have not used fertiliser before. For this reason it is proposed that some S. 0.5 million per annum be allocated for extension officers, to work on both cultivation and the organisation of marketing. This budget would have to be allocated for the four years 4–7 to have the required effects.

(c) *Ministry of Agriculture and Rural Development*
      (Chief Economist, Research Division)

The current market prices (in the Western Province) for the crops mentioned are shown below. We also show the import and export prices quoted at Port Janus. The transport cost from the Hauriendum area to the port is estimated to be S. 2.5/q.

PRICES (SOLDI PER QUINTAL)

	Local	Export	Import
Maize	50	—	—
Wheat	60	—	54
Oilseed	120	122	—

Fertiliser is available in the Western Region at S. 500 per ton. The wage rate for unskilled agricultural labour is fairly equal throughout the country, and is currently S. 6 per day.

The project as a whole looks reasonable to us, and would fit in with our general framework for agricultural development, but we would like to see a more detailed analysis before giving a final opinion. We think that we can fit the requirements for extension expenditure (mentioned by Cibus Research in their visit to this Ministry) into our operating budgets for the period mentioned. At present we have no extension programmes in the area.

(d) Ministry of Public Works
(Director, Planning and Budgeting Division)

The Ministry is prepared to support the project if economically feasible (although we feel that the whole matter might have been better decided within this Ministry), but it is clear that this will absorb a large proportion of our already small budget for this type of irrigation work in the next five-year plan. *Two* other projects, in the Southern and Northern Regions, would produce a positive NPV (according to our estimates) of S. 10 million and S. 5 million respectively, for roughly the same budget outlay, but would have to be cancelled if we go ahead with the Hauriendum project.

The wage rate currently paid for unskilled labour on public works projects is S. 10/day.

(e) National Planning Commission
(Director, Programming Section)

In reply to your request for information, we include the following standard parameters used on all major projects analysed by this Commission.

> Discount rate: 12% per annum
> Shadow wage for unskilled labour: $4/days

The official exchange rate is 1 Soldus (S) =US $0·4 but we feel that foreign exchange is rather scarce and the Commission has ruled that a 25 per cent 'markup' be placed on import or export prices when valuing public sector projects. The distribution of income by region is as follows:

	Income (S.m.)	Population (million)
Northern	1200	3
Southern	200	1
Eastern	1400	2
Western	1200	4
Nusquam	4000	10

PART II
THE PLANNING OF PUBLIC INVESTMENT

CHAPTER 8

INVESTMENT BY THE STATE

WHEN we discuss project appraisal and sectoral planning we are essentially talking about investment by the state, and although the criteria so developed are relevant to the application of (say) licensing rules for private foreign investment, it is the public sector that remains the main concern of the planner. In consequence, the individual project must be, and inevitably is, seen in the context of the public investment programme as a whole and, perhaps more importantly, of the role of this latter in economic development. To a certain extent, of course, these wider aims are expressed by the inclusion of external effects and the application of shadow prices within the decentralised cost–benefit framework. None the less, it is not possible to claim that this is enough to express national objectives completely, above all those related to structural change, because cost–benefit analysis is concerned with marginal adjustment to a given pattern of production, distribution and ownership.

It is, therefore, this broader aspect of public investment planning that is inadequately covered by the techniques of project appraisal which we have explored in Part I. Specifically, we have already found that three important issues were left unresolved. First, the setting of the Planning Discount Rate (which is discussed further on in this chapter) as the means of allocating public investment funds; second, the process by which project proposals are generated and related to intersectoral input requirements (which are among the topics of Chapter 9), particularly in relation to non-traded output; and third, the need for investment optimisation over time and space in relation to sets of projects rather than a single one (which is the specific topic of Chapter 10). Beyond these

there are a number of strategic issues in development planning
which throw considerable light upon what may appear at first sight
to be technical problems susceptible to improved microplanning
method (such as the 'choice of techniques') but which on further
examination turn out to involve far wider considerations: these
are taken up in Chapter 11. These topics, then, make up Part
II, which serves both to complement, and provide a framework
for, the methodology of project analysis itself.

In this chapter we shall be concerned with the role of the state
in the accumulation process, the general nature of the relationship between national plans and individual projects, and the
derivation of the planning discount rate as part of the procedure
for the allocation of public investment funds.

The State and the Accumulation Process

The essential analytical prelude to an understanding of the
problems of public investment planning in any economy is the
establishment of the nature of state participation in the process
of accumulation. This is not just an academic question, because in
a practical context unless policy on this matter is made specific
in a concrete form it is not really possible to define the extent of
the possible public investment programme, let alone work out its
most desirable form.

By the 'accumulation process' we mean the way in which, within a given structure of ownership of the means of production, the
surplus of output over the basic consumption needs of the work-
force is extracted, mobilised through financial institutions and
invested in the form of productive capacity. In practice, profit
and taxation are the main means of this extraction, although
surplus may be transferred from one sector to another in a market
economy through the price system: the most important examples
of this are the internal terms of trade, which shift surplus from
agriculture to industry through the relative prices of food and
manufactures, and the external terms of trade, which shift the
surplus from the primary export sector to industry through the
relative prices of raw material exports and imported industrial
inputs. The state can intervene in this aspect of the surplus
generation process in an 'institutional' manner by adjusting prices
(e.g. the exchange rate) or by directly controlling factors of
production such as the labour force. These activities are not our
concern here, however.

The public investment process involves, by definition, the expropriation by the state of some part of this surplus, through the taxation of profits and wages, through public enterprise savings, or through monetary emission. Borrowing, either domestic or foreign, only 'delays' this expropriation requirement by the term of the loan, of course. The effect of turning this ex-propriated surplus into fixed capital in the public sector* can logically be either an increase in total investment in the economy, or its redirection from one branch to another. The exact form and scale of the effect will depend upon the extent of state in-volvement in the accumulation process, and will in turn provide the essential premiss for the public investment planning procedure.

First, we can distinguish the case where the state plays a *support* role to the private sector, where its main activities are the provision of infrastructure and finance. The former activity covers transport facilities such as roads, basic inputs such as electricity and heavy industry such as steel. This is equivalent to the state acting as a 'committee chairman' for private capital, providing the large 'lumps' of investment that individual firms could not afford, but need in order to expand their own activities and make their own investments profitable. This may also mean a consider-able net subsidy to the users of the infrastructure, as it is usually provided free or run at a loss. The latter activity involves the participation of state development banks in the mobilisation of private saving and government development funds from one production sector to another (e.g. from agriculture to industry) or possibly from one social class to another (e.g. from small savers to large industrialists), as in the process of development savings are often in the hands of those not able to invest them directly in the most productive activities. Again, subsidy to borrowers way result from the low interest rates normally charged by develop-ment banks.

Second, we can distinguish the case where the state plays a *controlling* role in the economy, or at least in the 'corporate' sector,† and both infrastructure and final production fall within

*It is also used for *current* expenditure, of course, which is not our concern here, either.

†That is, organised enterprises coming under company legislation, and thus excluding artisans, petty traders, peasants and so on.

public sectors activities. The provision of roads, power and steel is then in support of other state enterprises, and the transfer of funds from one sector to another is internal to the budgeting process.

The relevant difference for our analysis, however, is that although both these roles involve massive programmes of state investment, the first 'support' role means that the private sector is still the main centre of profit and the determinant of the final production pattern, under the influence of market forces, while the second 'control' role means that the state controls both these functions directly. The implications for planning are clear: in the support case the provision of infrastructure and finance inevitably reflects the needs of the private sector rather than those of the economy as a whole, let alone the poorer members of the community. In other words, the economy is essentially 'unplanned' and state investment a reaction to events rather than a dynamic force in itself. Specifically, the implicit objective of such support may well be to increase profits in the private sector, rather than economic growth or redistribution. Direct state control of the corporate sector does at least permit the possibility of an integrated planning process and thus the achievement of wider economic aims through the restructuring of production.

When the concurrent political structures are brought into the analysis, the argument becomes stronger, even though such an exercise must remain speculative. It is reasonable to suppose that in cases where the 'support' role is maintained then the private sector (that is, both domestic and foreign capitalists) will have a dominant influence over the government in the matter of economic policy, and can impose the objective of private profitability on the public sector in principle or practice. In other words, the 'seriousness' with which the criteria discussed elsewhere in this book might be applied would be limited by the true objectives of the government or by the constraints put upon its putting its programmes into practice. Unfortunately this reservation applies to the great majority of countries in the Third World. Of course, the existence of state control, itself the consequence of a shift in the class composition of the state, may be a necessary condition for effective planning but by no means a sufficient one. Moreover, even though integrated planning may be applied, the objectives may still be such as to favour the bureaucratic and skilled classes, at the expense of the poor. The most important point, perhaps, is that considerations such as these cannot be ignored when discussing public investment: it cannot just simply be assumed that the state acts independently of social forces and for the greater good of the whole community, let alone its poorest members.

Projects and Plans

Given these reservations as to the relationship between the state and the rest of the economy, within the public sector budgeting process itself one of the key problems is the proper relationship between the individual project and overall planning strategy. We have already seen that the attempt to completely separate projects from the plan as a whole is misconceived because of the important parameter values that are thereby left unresolved – in other words, there is a positive need for a 'downward' flow of information. The 'upward' process of fitting the projects into the available budget is the topic of the methodological discussion in the next section of this chapter.

There has been in the past a certain amount of somewhat sterile argument among planners as to the relative merits of planning 'from the top down' as opposed to 'from the bottom up' – the former referring to the prior determination of the macroeconomic plan and the derivation of projects (i.e. investment requirements) therefrom, while the latter term refers to the identification of feasible projects and the building up of an aggregate plan from these elements. In practice, of course, the process is inevitably a circular one, involving both these steps. The public sector budget, which links plans to projects, will be *initially* drafted on the basis of aggregate estimates of the requirements of different branches, and *subsequently* adjusted according to the project proposals moving up through the system.

The first of these steps involves the 'working down' from aggregate estimates of production to the needs for intermediate inputs and the capacity to produce them on a 'branch' basis, and from this are derived the investment needs from average capital–output ratios. Then a first estimate of the aggregate capital expenditure requirement is worked out, which is compared with the estimated finance available from the government's own current account surplus, public enterprise profits, domestic borrowing and foreign loans or grants. This second step involves adjustment of the two totals both overall and possibly within the major administrative sectors such as mining, agriculture, industry and so on

The third step requires that more precise estimates of public investment requirements be built up from the pre-feasibility studies of planned projects. This goes on at the same time as the first step, and involves the application of the 'screening' methods of Chapter 9 and the 'rationing' methods of the next section of this chapter. The result will inevitably be different from that of the first and second stages, and will almost certainly imply higher expenditure, so that either postponement of projects or the acquisition of further capital funds will be necessary. Finally, a compromise is reached as the result of which the plan, the investment budget and the project set should be mutually *consistent*, and hopefully some way towards a feasible optimum as well.

The theoretical presentation of this 'circular' procedure (technically known as 'iteration') tends to underestimate the difficulties in practice,* which clearly place serious constraints on the freedom to achieve an optimal result. Quite apart from administrative weaknesses and the shortage of reliable information, the timing factor can be crucial. In the normal course of events, major projects will have a long gestation period, and thus for any one (say five-year) planning period, much of the capital funds for the period will have been committed by decisions made during the previous planning period, or even the one before that. In consequence, it would not be unusual for the uncommitted budget to be less than half the total at any one point in time. Thus, when the most 'pressing' new projects are added, the public investment budget may be somewhat inflexible, and the aggregate plan has to be pragmatically adjusted to it. As a result there often tends to be an inconsistency between the projects and the budget on the one hand, and the plan on the other!

The Theory of Allocation and the Planning Discount Rate

At the project level, the main way of allocating capital funds between one project and another is the discount rate. In other words, to the extent that the positive net present value is taken as

*For a description of and commentary on a fairly efficient public investment planning system, that of Peru, see chapter 6 of FitzGerald (1976a).

the criterion for accepting a project (and therefore the required amount of public funds are dedicated to it), the discount rate expresses the 'price' of those funds, and the internal rate of return of the project (its 'value') must exceed this 'price' to gain acceptance. A high planning discount rate means that less projects can 'get through' the planning office – that is, when funds are scarce they must be rationed out to the better projects among those available. This applies not only to a decentralised system of planning based mainly on individual projects, but also to a system where output in each branch is set centrally, because even the selection of a 'minimum cost of supply' solution requires the comparison of future with present costs through the discounting of the former to the present. Therefore, within the budgeting system, the discount rate plays an essential part in the allocation process.

The setting of the planning discount rate is not a matter of estimating a parameter which in some sense is determined by the economy (such as, say, the shadow wage rate) but rather requires a consideration of the way in which capital funds are allocated within the public sector and, more important, of the role of the state within the accumulation process. There are, indeed, two main approaches to the setting of the discount rate, which correspond to the broad differentiation of the economic role of the state that we have already outlined earlier in this chapter. These correspond to the 'support' and 'control' roles for the state, which suppose virtually complete state planning of the modern sector in the latter case and a more marginal role in the provision of infrastructure in the former.

The first of these roles underlies the original model for the discount rate, which to a great extent was adopted by most planners until about a decade ago. It is based on the assumption that the state, with its limited economic role and constrained tax base, must rely upon borrowing to sustain even infrastructure funding requirements. This may involve large amounts of overseas finance, but at the margin (i.e. the extra funds for the extra project) the source is almost inevitably borrowing from the domestic capital market.* The model then argues that expansion

---

*The interest rate on these loans is not a reliable indicator, naturally, as bonds are usually more or less forced on the banks. Incidentally,

in state borrowing reduces the savings of the private sector by a proportionate amount, and private investment as well. The economic opportunity cost of the funds obtained by the state is then simply the return on private capital at the margin; specifically, the planning rate of discount will be the increment of annual profits arising from an increase in private investment in the economy. Although some formidable statistical problems are involved, the principle is clear, and is based on profitability as a measure of the value of capital, with suitable adjustments for shadow prices and so on. This method is explained extremely clearly in Harberger (1972), and with some refinements for differing responses of the private capital market to public borrowing, by Marglin (1967). The major difficulty with this approach is that it ignores the social relationships (e.g. the power of capitalists to set wages) which are as important as 'efficiency' in determining profitability – a problem we have already encountered in Chapter 5. None the less, it does have a certain consistency with the 'support' role for the state, and it could be argued that the corresponding type of government might well believe private profitability to be the relevant measure of the cost of government funds. Broadly, this model would give a rate of discount (R) for planning independent of the budgeting process itself and equal to the product of the rate of growth of private profits $(\Delta P/P)$ and the proportion of profits in national income (P/Y) divided by the private investment rate (I/Y):

$$R = \frac{\Delta P}{I} = \frac{\Delta P}{P} \cdot \frac{P}{Y} \cdot \frac{Y}{I}$$

An essentially similar approach is suggested by Solow (1963) where the relationship between the capital–output ratio for the economy as a whole and the resulting increment of annual consumption (i.e. national income less savings) is taken as the basis of a 'social rate of discount', which is roughly the average productivity of investment at an aggregate level. Again, the difficulty is that this reduces the entire process of economic growth to a single determinant (ignoring factors such as export prices) and implies

the other marginal source is often inflationary monetary expansion, but it can be argued that this has a similar effect on domestic investment, which is presumably the point.

that to gain acceptance public projects must do at least as well as the average for investment as a whole.

The second and more recent method involves a different approach, supposing a dominant state sector within which total investment is based on determinate control over the mobilised surplus and constrained by the planned savings coefficient. Against this fixed total $(\bar{K})$ a collection of feasible projects is ranged (Figure 6). Depending upon the level of the planning discount rate (r), a larger or smaller number of projects will have

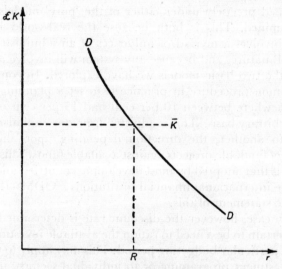

FIG. 6. Capital Budgeting

positive NPVs, and will thus produce different requirements (D) of capital funds. The optimal discount rate (R) is then the rate that exactly balances the requirements ('demand') with the available budget ('supply'). In this way, the total 'value' of public investment is maximised, and in fact the optimal discount rate emerges as the internal rate of return on the marginal project. 'Emerges' is an appropriate description, because the optimal rate is the result of an allocation procedure rather than the cause of it. It is not, therefore, a 'parameter' in quite the same way that the result of the first model is. The organisation of this form of budgeting is clearly crucial to the determination of the value of the planning discount rate, but the theoretical form could be equally satisfied either by the allocation of funds between projects already submitted to the central planning office (and recalculated there with different discount rates in order to establish the D function) or by the 'issuing' of a trial discount rate to the investment agencies themselves and adjusting this according to the resultant requests to the treasury for funds.* This latter is the general approach recommended in both OECD (1968) and UNIDO (1972).

In practice, the setting of the discount rate itself cannot be determined precisely under either of the 'pure' models we have just examined. This is both because the real-world budgeting process involves a myriad of influences of an administrative and 'political' nature, and because any system will involve an admixture of the two basic models we have explored. In consequence, the common procedure in practice is to set a planning discount rate somewhere between 10 per cent and 15 per cent on a more or less arbitrary basis. This is adjusted from one capital-budgeting period to another, the direction depending upon the relative balance of fundable projects against available funds. This practical solution is that adopted by most developing countries, and suggested by the international financial institutions – ODM (1972) gives a specific statement of this.

In any case, however the discount rate is determined, there is almost certain to be a need to ration the available investment funds within a particular budgeting period. This may apply to the whole state investment programme or to individual sectors, and results from the problem of the state not exercising sufficient control over the surplus to secure the desired rate of accumulation. In consequence, it is necessary to ensure that the available funds $(\overline{K})$ are allocated among the feasible projects (i) in such a way as to maximise the economic value derived from them – in other words, so as to obtain the greatest 'aggregate NPV'. The method used is to calculate the *cost–benefit ratio* in relation to the portion of the relevant budget (K_i) used on the project. This 'CBR' is normally expressed as

$$M_i = \frac{B_i - C_i'}{K_i}$$

*We shall take this up again in Chapter 12.

where the discounted costs (C'_i), to be set against the discounted benefits (B_i), are those *other* than the discounted capital cost (K_i) from the budget, so that total costs (C_i) are

$$C_i = C'_i + K_i$$

Therefore, we could write

$$M_i = \frac{\text{NPV}_i + K_i}{K_i} = \frac{\text{NPV}_i}{K_i} + 1$$

and so for projects with a positive NPV it is automatically true that

$$M_i > 1$$

The 'CBR criterion' is applied by ranking a set of project proposals coming under the relevant budgetary head in decreasing order of their CBR. The choice of projects made from the list in this order, up to the point where the budgetary allocation is filled, will result in the 'NPV sum' from the allocation being maximised. As long as all the projects chosen have CBRs greater than unity, they will of course be acceptable on the NPV criterion as well.

To take an example, a set of projects might have the properties shown in the table, the last two columns being derived from the second and third.

Name	NPV	K	CBR	Ranking
	($ m.)	($ m.)	($ m.)	
A	238	70	2.4	2
B	150	60	1.5	4
C	155	50	2.1	3
D	328	80	3.1	1
E	336	120	1.8	5

With a total budget allocation $(\overline{K})$ of $200 million, we would choose projects D, A and C (in that order), yielding a total NPV sum of $721 million, higher than any other combination: the choice of project E (the one with the highest NPV) would lead with project D to a total yield of only $664 millions from the same budget of $200 million. In cases where the chosen projects do not 'fit' precisely into the overall allocation, then some adjustment to either the former or latter will be necessary.

Further Points

In this chapter we have put forward a complex and somewhat inconclusive argument in order to place the determination of the discount rate in the relevant context. This is necessary in order to avoid a simplistic approach to the problem, which might propose a technique without reference to its implications for the economic role of the state. In particular, the attempt to introduce the 'new' methodology (i.e. the second of our two models) in the majority of Third World economies, where the state plays only a supportive role, is clearly misguided. That the major international financial institutions should apparently be doing this can only be explained by the possibly inconsistent aims of giving public support to socially desirable development planning while continuing to effectively promote the 'mixed' economy. It should be recognised, none the less, that the problem of the discount rate is necessarily a controversial one precisely because it requires a precise definition of the proposed economic articulation of the state.

Relevant reading which covers the exact topic of this chapter is difficult to find, even though all texts on development planning necessarily touch upon it, albeit implicitly. For the role of the public sector in development, see Sachs (1964), upon which the analysis outlined in this chapter is based, being developed further for the Latin American case in FitzGerald (1976b). Kindleberger (1965) and Baran (1957) exemplify conflicting views on this topic, corresponding to 'conservative' and 'radical' viewpoints, respectively. On the budgeting process, probably Millward (1971) is the most useful for the general principles, while Caiden and Wildavsky (1974) have a good analysis of experience in developing countries. On the specific issue of the discount rate, we have already pointed out that Harberger (1972) and Marglin (1967) represent the 'borrowing' approach, while OECD (1968) and UNIDO (1972) propose the 'rationing' method.

CHAPTER 9

SECTORAL PLANNING

ONE of the major problems of analysing projects is, as we have seen in Part I, the fact that appraisal methods in themselves may not give a satisfactory method of relating a project to the rest of a production sector or to the economy as a whole. The detailed analysis of external costs and benefits of a single project discussed in Chapter 3 is clearly helpful, but it is essentially a marginal exercise and cannot help in the determination of optimal project choice. In part this objective is the subject of Chapter 10, where optimal investment allocation methods are explored that relate one project to another in time or space, allowing choice from a large number of possible alternatives. None the less, it is probably in the area of 'project generation' that the major practical and theoretical problems arise. Practical, because in normal practice there is generally a lack of alternative project proposals in a suitable state for appraisal at any one point in time, which is not the same as the number already decided upon and awaiting finance – these alone often exceed available funds, as we have seen in Chapter 8. In consequence, projects turn up for appraisal in a haphazard manner, or else key shortages are identified too late, and single versions are put together on engineering criteria alone. Theoretical, because there exists, as we saw in Chapter 4, a major difficulty in the setting of the value of non-traded output from a project, a difficulty that can only be resolved by abandoning the attempt at valuation on a marginal basis and instead setting output of these commodities in terms of national or local requirements. This requires the planned, or at least the rationally anticipated, production of these commodities in a coordinated fashion.

111

It is to resolve both these problems that *sectoral planning* has become an integral part of the public investment allocation process. By 'sectoral planning' in this context we mean the anticipation of requirements in particular key branches of production (especially basic industrial inputs and essential consumer goods) and the programmed expansion of productive capacity in such a way as to secure adequate supply and avoid the emergence of 'bottlenecks'. Beyond this 'passive' anticipation of requirements, an 'active' role for sectoral planning involves the deliberate development of a particular production structure, such as that implied by import-substituting industrialisation or the attainment of self-sufficiency in foodgrains.

The exact nature of the methods used is as much a matter of practical experience as theoretical principle, but we can separate out three approaches that are actually in general use and which together can be said to compose the pragmatic approach to sectoral planning: the simple 'materials balance' which forms the foundation both of 'project screening' and the more sophisticated apparatus of input–output analysis. These, in turn, are complemented by the new methods of mathematical programming that are the subject of Chapter 10.

Materials Balances

The simplest, and in some ways still the most effective, technique for sectoral planning is by the use of material balances. The method requires a minimum of data, and is extensively used both in centrally planned systems such as the USSR and in 'mixed' economies such as Pakistan and India.

The first step is to set up the actual balance for previous years. This, in effect, describes the supply and demand flows for the commodity in question, such as cement or rice. On the supply side, we have domestic production, imports and stock changes: the first two are readily available and the third may be estimated (or perhaps ignored). On the demand side, we have domestic consumption and exports. The second is known, of course, and the first may be estimated from the materials balance itself, in which case it is called 'apparent consumption'. As an example, we can take the analysis of cement in a particular country. The balances of production and consumption must be analysed on a national and regional basis, to establish 'requirements' which in the future must be met from imports or an increase in domestic output.

MATERIALS BALANCE FOR CEMENT ('000 TONS)

	1971	1976
Domestic production	800	1000
Imports	200	200
Changes in stocks*	—	+20
Total Supply	1000	1220
Domestic consumption	900	1100
Exports	100	120
Total Demand	1000	1220

*+ = a decline in stocks

In this case, there is a net deficit of domestic production with respect to domestic consumption, but both imports and exports are taking place. This might appear to be inconsistent as it stands, and a regional breakdown of the materials balance would be helpful, in which case interregional transfers will be included.

REGIONAL MATERIALS BALANCE FOR CEMENT, 1976 ('000 TONS)

	North	South	Total
Regional production	800	200	1000
Imports	–	200	200
Stock changes	+ 20	–	20
Regional transfers	−100	+100	–
Total Supply	720	500	1220
Regional consumption	600	500	1100
Exports	120	–	120
Total Demand	720	500	1220

The position is now clear; the South region is in deficit, importing both from the North and from abroad, while the North is in overall surplus, exporting abroad and to the South.

The next step is to construct the materials balance for 1981. The forecasts of total demand are based on consumption and exports projections: the demand for cement is an intermediate demand, and will be based on, for example, the growth targets for construction, while consumption demand (e.g. for rice) would be based on projected income growth and an income elasticity, in the way discussed in Chapter 1. The object of micro-planning is to adjust the supply structure, through a combination of imports (M) and increased productive capacity (Q). In this case, we calculate cement requirements forecasts from the index of construction activity included in the Five Year Plan (1978–82), which indicates that the volume of construction (and thus the cement required, assuming that the 'technical coefficient' – that is, the volume of cement per unit of construction – is constant) will increase by 23 per cent between 1976 and 1981.

CEMENT PLAN ('000 TONS)

	1976	1980
Supply: Production	1000	$1000+Q$
Imports	200	M
Stocks	$+20$	—
Total	1220	$1000+Q+M$
Demand:	1220	1500

We now have a planning equation:

$$Q+M=500$$

That is, an extra 500,000 tons of cement are needed by 1981 which must either be imported or produced domestically.

We thus have a problem in project appraisal to consider. Are we to build extra plant for domestic production or to import? If we expand domestically, should we plan for 300,000 tons, or 500,000 tons (to eliminate imports altogether), or even more? Should the plant be in the South (the deficit region) or in the North? We can then apply the methodology described in Part I directly, having made use of the materials balance analysis as the essential part of project screening.

Project Screening

The need for a specific 'project screening' procedure before project appraisal proper arises because it is normal for project 'ideas' to be initiated at a comparatively low level of the state apparatus (if not outside it) and during their slow rise through the planning system of an agency and responsible ministry they acquire not only a technical feasibility study but often a totally inadequate economic appraisal as well. By the time that this one variant has reached the central planning office in the form of a specific ministerial proposal* it will have accumulated considerable bureaucratic momentum, and given the inevitable pressure for acceptance once the design has been carried out (at some considerable cost) there may be little option but to accept the project as it stands.

There is a real need, therefore, for an administrative system that allows for more feasibility studies in general, and earlier intervention by the planning office in particular, than is usually the case. The three key stages in the 'project cycle' are the pre-feasibility study, the feasibility study, and the project appraisal proper. Part I of this book has been devoted to this last stage, but if (as is common) the feasibility study has determined the product type, location, plant size and input requirements on engineering or (at best) market-price criteria, then it is amost impossible to rework, let alone radically change the project. Therefore it is only at the pre-feasibility stage that modification is possible, and the application of economy-wide criteria really effective. For example, it is only here that the shadow wage rate can be applied so as to shift project choice towards employment creation or linkage criteria applied in order to promote intersectoral integration – both of which require the processing of fundamentally different project concepts.

The essential procedure for project screening, which should be the basis of the pre-feasibility stage of public investment planning, starts with the forecasting of future requirements of goods and services within the materials balance framework we have just examined, and the comparison of the result with the existing output structure to provide an estimate of the key 'gaps'. These should be estimated for as many products and regions as possible,

---

*Probably in the hope of 'rubber stamping'.

integrated through the input–output method we shall examine later. This will not cover all cases, of course, and many projects will still be initiated at an agency level. The crucial requirement is that the central planning office intervene* at a very early stage, through its sectoral and regional divisions, to analyse in approximate terms the ways in which the shortfall can be covered. This requires small teams of trained engineers and economists working together, as well as a considerable amount of standardised data on production costs and shadow prices *specifically gathered for this purpose*, along with lists of all known project opportunities. This last item should be particularly concerned with natural resources, transport links and other 'locality specific' 'proposals, and requires considerable research on project identification and updating. None the less, this type of procedure is the only way in which the methods of Part I can be applied with any real effect.†

For instance, in many cases the cheapest method of supply will depend upon the scale of production, and thus upon the size of the gap to be covered. A particular case is import-substitution where the immediate issue (if more general 'infant industry' criteria are not involved) is whether domestic production or imports is a cheaper method of obtaining the required supply of the commodity. The object of project screening in this case is to work with standardised cost functions (based on census data, company accounts and special studies) to produce a rough estimate of which alternative is the cheaper, both immediately and over the rest of the planning period. For the purpose of illustration, we may assume that the cost-of-production function for domestic installation (C_d) is made up of a fixed charge (a) relating to installation costs (plant and infrastructure) combined with a variable operating cost (b) related to the volume of production (x):

*This will result in considerable resistance from the individual ministries, as it reduces their effective control over investment, and may well require specific legislation.

†Moreover, however expensive this may seem, it will be cheap compared to the losses from bad project choices. For example, a 20 percent saving achieved by relocating a road project costing $1 million (a small project by todays standards) would easily cover the wages of a dozen project analysts!

$$C_d = a + bx$$

The cost of importing (C_m) is given by the international price (p):

$$C_m = p.x$$

The two can be graphed (Figure 7), from which it can be seen that until the 'gap' in the materials balance reaches a certain value $(\bar{x})$, it is cheaper to continue importing the good in question. The same analysis can be shown on a unit-cost basis, in which case we have, for domestic production,

$$\frac{C_d}{x} = \frac{a}{x} + b$$

and for importing,

$$\frac{C_m}{x} = p$$

Import-substitution (i.e. domestic production) is justified where

$$p > \frac{a}{x} + b$$

so that the critical level of demand is

$$\bar{x} = \frac{a}{p - b}$$

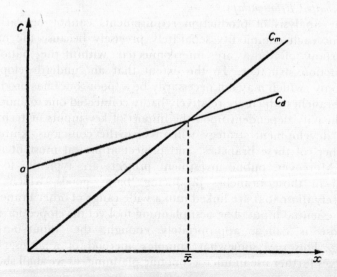

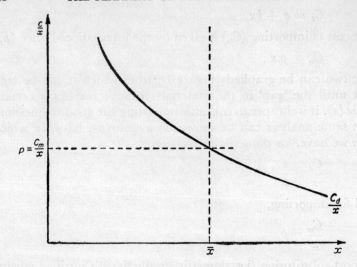

FIG. 7: Import Substitution

Although we have presented this analysis in terms of project selection at any one point in time, it is also extremely useful in the placing of projects in temporal sequence, as we shall see in the next chapter.

Input–output Relationships

The analysis of production requirements cannot be carried out for each commodity separately precisely because the most important of those are interconnected within the national production structure. To the extent that an 'underdeveloped' economy (which may not necessarily be a 'poor' one) has production branches which are relatively badly connected one to another and heavily dependent upon the import of key inputs or technology, development strategy will involve the conscious 'knitting together' of these branches, and project appraisal must fit into this. Moreover, public investment projects are typically to be found in those branches producing 'basic' goods, which are precisely those that are linked into a wide range of other branches as an essential input. The best planning tool yet developed for this purpose is called, appropriately enough, the 'input–output table'. This is a somewhat complex method of analysis, but deserves further use in microeconomic planning, as we shall show.

A full input–output table contains about fifty columns and rows in a typical case for a developing economy, and enters into particular detail for the industrial sector, as this is the sector for which the economic census (upon which the table is based) is most precise – the agricultural and service sectors being less 'organised' and more difficult to find reliable data for. The table below shows, in concentrated form, the usual structure.

SUMMARY INPUT–OUTPUT TABLE ($BILLIONS)

OUTPUT / INPUT	Agriculture	Industry	Services	Sub-Total	Investment	Consumption	Exports	TOTAL OUTPUT
Agriculture	4	3	3	10	4	32	6	52
Industry	2	3	3	8	8	11	1	28
Services	2	3	4	9	2	17	2	30
Sub-total	8	9	10	27	14	60	9	110
Labour	30	6	12	48				
Imports	—	9	1	10				
Surplus	14	4	7	25				
TOTAL INPUTS	52	28	30	110				

In this example, the important relationship of (say) 'industry' to the rest of the economy is established through purchases (inputs) from and sales (outputs) to the rest of the economy. 'Intersectoral' sales are made to agriculture ($2 billion), to enterprises within the industrial sector itself ($3 billion) and services ($3 billion), giving a sub-total of $8 billion. In addition, there are sales of investment goods ($8 billion), consumer goods ($11 billion) and exports ($1 billion), the whole giving total output of $28 billion. Intersectoral purchases are made from agriculture ($3 billion), from enterprises within industry (3 billion) and services ($3 billion), which with the purchase of labour ($6 billion), imported inputs ($9 billion) and the 'surplus' item – which includes tax, depreciation and profit – gives us total inputs of $28 billion. In this way, the matrix is balanced* for each sector, the informa-

*Incidentally, the sum of investment, consumption and the trade balance $(I+C+X-M)$ is the gross national product of course– $73 billion in this case.

tion coming from the transactions reported by enterprises in the national economic census, and relating to the situation in that year.

The input–output table as it stands, then, is just a statement of the intersectoral transactions in any one year. The key assumption in its use as a tool in sectoral planning is that the 'technical coefficients' remain stable. By this is meant the amount of a certain input needed for the output of one unit of a commodity: in the example, each unit of 'industrial' output is assumed to directly require 0.107 units $(3 \div 28)$ of 'agricultural' inputs to produce it. On this assumption, which is equivalent to that of no economies of scale nor discontinuities in the cost function, the requirements for the output of any given branch of intermediate production can be estimated from the forecasts of demand for the final product derived in the national plan. This involves more than the direct application of the appropriate technical coefficient because there are indirect agricultural inputs to industry as the service sector itself takes some agricultural inputs. The computational method required to solve this problem is called 'matrix inversion', and is essentially equivalent to solving a set of simultaneous equations* – a matter that need not concern us here as the inversion is normally carried out by statisticians in the central planning office. In the case of this example, each unit of industrial output requires, directly and indirectly, 0.136 units of agricultural output.

In practice, the input–output table is generally much more detailed, and in particular it normally allows the requirements of basic products such as steel, cement or electric power to be traced through to their final use in products for consumption, investment or export. Thus, if forecasts of these latter can be derived from the aggregate economic plan or individual projects, then the total requirements of (say) steel, cement and electric power can be estimated too. These calculations have two functions in project analysis. First, the forecast of requirements derived, or even their present levels, can be compared with the present supply conditions and lead into the appraisal of a supply project in the way discussed earlier in this chapter. Second, the structure of input costs can be used as the basis for calculating the shadow cost of non-traded

*But see Dorfman *et al.* (1958).

inputs in the manner explained in Chapter 4. The input–output table, therefore, is an important way of integrating project appraisal to the planning process as a whole.

Tinbergen has developed a *semi-input–output* method which, while it is considerably more simple, does allow for the necessary linkages ('complementary relationships') to be included. The relevant intersectoral relationships are handled by assuming that input changes are directly proportional to output changes, while the effect of increased incomes on the sector as a whole is assumed to be linear. Each 'international' (i.e. traded goods) sector is treated independently, and linkages need only be allowed for in the case of 'domestic' (i.e. non-traded goods) sectors.* Thus the international sectors need not be directly linked, although the components of a production group must be considered as a whole. In Tinbergen's words:

> An expansion of the weaving industry does not necessarily imply a corresponding expansion in the spinning industry–the yarns required can be imported. Whether a corresponding expansion in spinning is also attractive is something that has to be considered separately. (1967)

Projects in each production group (the 'investment bundle') should be coordinated, and the semi-input–output model will indicate the possibilities for investment and the effects of the project on other branches.

Further Points

The methods of sectoral planning discussed in this chapter must form a part of a much wider process of national planning, in the way discussed in Chapter 8, if they are to have any claim to be 'planning' as opposed to the programmed anticipation of the needs of the market. Above all, in a fully planned system, the pattern of final output and domestic supply of consumption goods – from which all the requirements in intermediate sectors, and thus project possibilities, flow – is determined in relation to the needs of

---

*In technical terms, the number of unknowns and equations will be equal to the number of *domestic* sectors, and thus much smaller than in the case of a full input–output method.

the population and not by market forces. Beyond this, the methods of materials balance and project screening as articulated through input–output analysis do depend upon the assumption of linearity – the absence of economies of scale – and work within an approach that searches for 'efficiency' rather than 'optimality'. Both these shortcomings are to some extent overcome by the 'optimal investment' methods discussed in the next chapter, but at the cost of isolating a particular production branch from the rest of the economy, which is the greater strength of the input–output methods. Some advance has been made in the inclusion of dynamic factors (particularly the changing values of the technical coefficients over time as technology progresses) and scale economies within the input–output framework, but this has not been applied in developing countries at an operational level as yet. None the less, the steady improvement of statistical information over the past two decades is probably of as much, if not more, importance than the development of method, both because the latter has tended to outstrip the former and because the direct examination of this sort of data helps to indicate 'gaps' in the productive structure and thus generate logical project possibilities, in many ways the crucial constraint on effective planning.

Reading on materials balances and project screening is somewhat scarce, but Bettelheim (1959) and Lewis (1966) respectively are as good as any. In contrast, the literature on input–output analysis is vast, but as introductory reading Cameron (1968) is extremely useful, and Eckaus (1973) contains an exposition of the advances just mentioned. The semi-input–output method is described in Tinbergen (1967), while the application to regional analysis is explained in Isard (1960) and the specific problems of industrial planning (where intersectoral linkages are of most importance) in Sutcliffe (1971) and Soza (1974). Finally, on the issues of sectoral balance and integration of the productive structure, see Hirschman (1958) and Griffin and Enos (1971).

CHAPTER 10

OPTIMAL INVESTMENT MODELS

In the previous chapter we examined empirical methods by which projects could be selected and placed within the sectoral plan. These methods attempt to secure a *consistent* project choice, in the sense that they promote the overall sectoral or national planning objectives. However, public investment planning should ideally be not only consistent but *optimal* – that is, involving the best of all the alternative solutions to a problem. This implies the maximisation of the sum of the net present values of a set of projects, which will determine project choices (i.e. individual capacity expansions) in terms of the requirements of a system rather than their individual merits. The process of optimisation should, in principle, involve the comparison of a very large number of project alternatives, each with its peculiar features and problems, and thus be a tedious and costly business – in terms of both time and resources – despite the methods of 'project screening'. The only practical procedure, then, is to simplify the production functions, and the constraints that act upon them, to the point where they are susceptible to solution by mathematical or 'numerical' (i.e. computer-based) methods. But this in turn means a degree of simplification and loss of detail that necessarily reduces the usefulness of the result as an exact description of the best practical solution. Optimisation models, then, are only a method of indicating the approximate nature of the best allocation, around which practical project alternatives can be examined.

The existence of economies of scale and indivisibilities lies at the root of the need for investment programming. Both the former (which is equivalent to falling unit costs with increased production) and the latter (due to productive capacity existing in specific 'sizes') imply that a scale of production greater than that immediately required at a certain time or place may be optimal.* In this case there is a need for the planning of investment over time and space, which will also occur where different production processes are combined or compete for the same resources. The aim of this chapter is to explore the relevant methods in a simple way so as to indicate their nature and relevance, leaving detailed methodology to the further reading listed in the last paragraph.

Allocation in Time

The optimal allocation of investment over time involves the maximisation of an objective function in terms of the discounted sum of costs and benefits over time and where the relevant variables are the scale and timing of the investment undertaken. Therefore, in terms of the net resource flow (x_t) and investment (k_t) in each year (t), the maximand is

$$Z = \sum_{t=0}^{n} \frac{x_t}{(1+r)^t} - \sum_{t=0}^{n} \frac{k_t}{(1+r)^t}$$

and the extremal condition is simply

$$\frac{\partial Z}{\partial k_t} = 0 \qquad \text{for } t = 0 \dots n$$

However, in practice we cannot establish the objective function in a simple form, and we find that two particular problems are those of timing and scale, both arising from the indivisibility of investment. In other words, we cannot just add to productive capacity year by year in the exact amount needed, because in the case of (say) road improvement we either asphalt the road or we do not, while in the case of chemical production very small plant increments involve high-cost production.

We shall start by examining the *timing* of a road project, where the traffic (X_t) is increasing over time (t). The benefits relate to

*If this were not so, most planning problems would disappear, because capacity expansion could be undertaken in small steps exactly when and where required, without raising unit costs.

unit cost savings (b), so that total benefits (B_t) are given by

$$B_t = bX_t$$

We must subtract the capital cost of the road (K) and the annual unit maintenance costs (a), giving total annual operating costs (C_t):

$$C_t = aX_t$$

The Net Present Value $(\mathcal{Z})$ of the project is given by

$$\mathcal{Z} = \sum_{t=T}^{N+T} \frac{(b-a)X_t}{(1+r)^t} - \frac{K}{(1+r)^T}$$

N = project life
r = discount rate
T = date of installation

This is at a maximum* where

$$rK = (b-a)X_T$$

that is, when the cost of bringing the investment (K) forward by one year (rK) is equal to the traffic benefits $(b-a)$ for that year. The traffic level at that point is given by

$$X_T = \frac{rK}{b-a}$$

This can be solved for quite general cost parameters and 'threshold' traffic levels determined for certain types of road improvement.

An example will probably clarify this problem. Let us suppose the following values for the symbols:

r = 10 per cent per annum
K = $50,000 per mile
b = 15 cents per vehicle-mile
a = 5 cents per vehicle-mile

Then

$$X_T = \frac{0.1 \times 50,000}{0.1}$$
$$= 50,000 \text{ vehicles/annum}$$

---

*That is, where $d\mathcal{Z}/dT = 0$, the solution to this being the equality given.

from which we can derive a 'rule of thumb' of the form 'pave the road if more than 150 vehicles a day use it'. If the appropriate discount rate were 15 per cent rather than 10 per cent, then the appropriate traffic level would be 75,000 vehicles per annum. If we had a growth forecast for traffic, then we could express this as an actual date, and thus construct a forward plan for the road investment.

The other aspect of 'dynamic' choices are those between plants of a different *scale*. Supposing we find that the capital costs of plant decline with scale (even though unit operating costs are the same) should we invest in large plants that are half-empty for a time or go for small-scale plant? In this sort of problem it is usual to express the objective as cost-minimisation (rather than the maximisation of benefits less costs) for a stated supply requirement, as the benefits from this supply are common to all the alternatives examined.

We shall examine a specific example first, and then generalise the result. Suppose we have a situation where demand for caustic soda is growing at some 100,000 tons/annum and we have the choice between building plant of 0.5 million tons and 1.0 million tons capacity. These will satisfy demand growth for 5 and 10 years respectively, and cost £4.0 million and £6.3 million. If the two-plant policy is pursued, plant is built in Year 0 and Year 5; while the one-plant policy would involve installation in Year 0 only.

	Cost of two-plant policy* (£m.)	Cost of one-plant policy (£m.)
Discount rate: 10%	6.48	6.30
15%	6.00	6.30

At 10 per cent discount rate, then, the one-plant policy is best, while the two-plant policy is preferable at a 15 per cent rate. Thus the higher the discount rate, the less attractive the large-scale plant becomes. In other words, the greater the cost of capital, the more expensive it becomes to maintain excess capacity.

*In the 10 per cent case the arithmetic is $4.0 (1+0.621) = 6.48$, and in the 15 per cent case $4.0 (1+0.497) = 6.00$

In formal terms, we can set out the problem as:

Cost of constructing in one stage,

$$K_1 = A_1$$

Cost of constructing in two stages,

$$K_2 = A_2 + \frac{A_3}{(1+r)^T} \qquad \begin{array}{l} T = \text{date of installation of} \\ \text{second plant} \end{array}$$

Supposing a linear* demand growth is given by

$$X_t = X_0 (1 + st)$$

so that the time taken (T) to fill the first of the small plants' capacity (Q) is given by

$$X_0 \, sT = Q$$

then

$$T = \frac{Q}{X_0 s}$$

so that the condition for choosing the one-stage rather than the two-stage process is that

$$K_1 < K_2$$

$$A_1 < A_2 + \frac{A_3}{(1+r)^T} = A_2 + \frac{A_3}{(1+r)^{Q/X_0 s}}$$

The 'solution' can be expressed in terms of the critical demand growth-rate (s) determined by

$$\frac{Q}{X_0 s} \cdot \log\ (1+r) = \log \left\{ \frac{A_3}{A_1 - A_2} \right\}$$

The higher the growth rate, the more attractive the one-plant policy, as the excess capacity is eliminated more rapidly. In the illustrative example above of the caustic soda plant, with the 10 per cent discount rate the one-plant policy will be justified as long as

---

*An exponential growth rate is not difficult to handle, either.

$$sX_0 > Q \cdot \frac{\log{(1+r)}}{\log\left\{\dfrac{A_3}{A_1 - A_2}\right\}}$$

$$= 86,000$$

In other words, so long as demand grows at a rate of at least 86,000 tons a year over the ten years, then the one–plant policy is preferable.

The development of this sort of analysis in a more sophisticated and mathematical form is known as 'dynamic programming', the 'dynamic' aspect referring not only to the fact that time is involved but also that the investment requirement for one time-period will depend on decisions made for previous periods and thus cannot be optimised separately – that is, on a single-project basis.

Allocation in Space

The theoretical principle underlying spatial allocation analysis* is essentially similar to that for allocation in time – the existense of indivisibilities and scale economies.   In other words, if production facilities were infinitely divisible and there were no scale economies, then every community, however small, could be entirely self-sufficient. In practice, of course, resources are located in specific places, there are considerable scale economies in industry, and many facilities (such as trunk roads) cannot be divided up at all.   In contrast to the dynamic analysis, the distinguishing feature is the cost of transport as opposed to the discounting of the future, to link together the parts of the production system to be optimised.   In consequence, the general objective is usually expressed in terms of maximising the net resource flow (x_i) at each centre (i) less the cost (y_{ij}) of transporting inputs and outputs between one centre (i) and another (j):

$$Z = \sum_{i=1}^{n} x_i - \sum_{i,j=1}^{n} y_{ij}$$

*This should not be confused with 'spatial location theory', which is concerned with the actual location choices of firms and communities, depending on market forces. Nor are we able to enter into the complexity of spatial planning in its full sense (e.g. urban plans); here we are concerned with the planning of production within a certain branch.

In practice, we have the twin problems of scale and location, which both introduce indivisibilities into the objective function, as there are a limited number of alternative plant sizes and locations to be considered.

Suppose we have two towns (C and D) with equal demand (Q) for cement; we can either build one large plant (capacity $2Q$) at C (annual capital charge a_1) or have two plants (annual capital charge a_2) one at C and one at D. As far as these capital charges are concerned, scale economies will give

$$a_1 < 2a_2$$

If we build the one large plant at C, we will have to incur a transport cost (z) for the shipment of Q tons from C to D. Total costs are now:

for one plant $a_1 + zQ$
for two plants $2a_2$

and a two-plant policy will be justified only if

$$2a_2 < a_1 + zQ$$

A practical example would be

$$a_1 = £6.3\text{m.}$$
$$a_2 = £4.0\text{m.}$$
$$Q = 0.5\text{m. tons}$$

Then the two-factory policy is only justified if

$$6.3 + 0.5\ z > 2(4.0)$$
$$z > £3\cdot4/\text{ton}$$

and if we know the freight costs per ton-mile (f), then we can work out the critical distance (d) as:

$$d = \frac{z}{f}$$

so that if

$$f = £0.02/\text{ton-mile}$$

then the minimum separation of towns C and D for a two-plant policy to be justified is

$$d_{\min} = \frac{3.4}{0.02} = 170 \text{ miles}$$

In this way, but with more sophisticated 'maps' of possible plant locations and transport networks between them, a minimum-cost programme can be worked out for and entire region or country. This involves 'spatial programming', the spatial element referring not only to the fact that space and thus transport costs are involved but also that the investment requirement for one location will depend on decisions as to other locations and thus cannot be optimised separately – that is, on a single-project basis.

Programming Models

The solution of complex allocation problems, involving not only a large number of separate processes but also multiple constraints upon the production process, requires the construction of 'allocation models' and the application of 'mathematical programming' to their solution. In reality, this only means an extension of the sort of exercises we have just examined, but expressed in a form that allows for their solution by computer. This in turn permits an enormous extension of the scale of the problem analysed.

The three crucial components of any programming model are the explicit definition and expression in mathematical form of the 'maximand', the 'functions' and the 'constraints'. The functions (f_i) relate the variables (x_j) in such a way as to express the production, benefit and cost relations in a mathematical form. A function for sales might relate price (p) with output (x) thus:

$$f(p,x) = p.x$$

The constraints (g) state the limits upon the value of any variable or sum of variables. Thus a constraint upon traffic (x) down a certain rail-route of a given capacity (g) would be expressed as

$$x \leqslant g$$

Finally, the maximand involves the maximisation of the objective function, itself the combination of functions, subject to the relevant constraints:

$$Z = \sum_{i,j} f_i (x_j)$$
$$\text{subject to } x_j \leqslant g_j$$

A specific case might be the maximisation of revenue for a specific rail-route with operating costs (c):

$$\text{maximise } \mathcal{Z} = p.x - c(x)$$
$$\text{subject to } x \leqslant g$$

But of course any real problem will involve a multitude of variables, functions and constraints.

The first method to be developed* for handling problems in mathematical planning was *linear programming*, and it is still the fundamental one. Its basic characteristic is that the functional relationships, and thus the maximand and the constraints, are linear. This makes the solutions relatively simple, even though a lot of data may have to be processed. The best way to explain the method is probably to explore a concrete example, and we shall take the case of choosing the best cropping pattern for the land area coming under an irrigation scheme.

The alternative crops are wheat and rice, and the total land area is to be sown to some combination of the two. The two crops differ in yield (i.e. tons per hectare), water requirements (i.e. centimetres per hectare), variable inputs (i.e. labour, fertiliser, machinery, etc.) and price. The object is to maximise net income (sales less variable inputs) subject to the overall constraints imposed by the availability of land and water, and the key variables are the areas sown to wheat and rice, respectively. This is a suitable problem for linear programming because both production and input requirement of each crop are directly proportionate to the area sown to it.

Suppose that we have the following data for the production of the two crops:

	Wheat	Rice
Yield: tons per hectare	1	2
Price: rupees per ton	140	80
Water needs: cm per ha	10	40
Other inputs: rupees/ha	80	40
Total land available $(\bar{L})$	2000 ha	
Total water available $(\bar{W})$	40,000 ha-cm	

---

*During the Second World War, in relation to complex logistics problems, although precedence is disputed by the United States and USSR.

We can now set up the functions (Figure 8) in terms of the land sown to wheat (X_1) and rice (X_2). Starting with the total land needed (L) we have obviously

$$L = X_1 + X_2$$

and for the total water requirements, similarly

$$W = 10.Z_1 + 40.X_2$$

The constraints on these requirements being

$$L \leqslant 2000 = \bar{L}$$
$$W \leqslant 40{,}000 = \bar{W}$$

The objective is to maximise the total income arising from the combined production of the two crops, subject to these constraints, the availability of the land and water resources being taken as given and not costed separately.* The sales per hectare will be the yield multiplied by the price, 140 and 160 rupees per hectare for wheat and rice, respectively, from which is deducted the variable input cost for each, giving the net income function (Y):

$$Y = X_1(140 - 80) + X_2(160 - 40)$$
$$= 60.X_1 + 120.X_2$$

So in formal terms, the problem is now:

maximise $Y = f(X_1, X_2)$ with respect to X_1, X_2 subject to $L \leqslant \bar{L}$ and $W \leqslant \bar{W}$.

The best way to illustrate the procedure for solution is by graphical exposition. The first step is to show the constraints on a graph. These are the equations:

$$X_1 + X_2 = 2000$$
$$\text{and } 10.X_1 + 40.X_2 = 40{,}000$$

while the existence of these constraints means that production (that is, a choice of combination of X_1 and X_2) is only possible

---

*They could be included in the cost equations, but would be the same for all project alternatives, and thus would not affect the outcome. If the land and water have no alternative use, then their joint value is the NPV of the project, of course (see Chapter 5).

within the area $ABCO$. It can simply be shown, moreover, that one or the other (cranmore, A, B or C) must be the most efficient solution, if either one or other of both the resources is being fully used. The next step is to map out the net income function of the investor who is trying to maximise. This is done by drawing a number of 'equal-income' lines on the same chart, each representing the different combinations of the variables x_1, x_2, that correspond to a particular income level:

$$z = 10x_1 + 10x_2$$

The object of the exercise is to attain the highest possible level of income whilst remaining within the constraints or the availability of the two resources. Given x_1, we then the super-imposition of the two graphs reveals that the B corner relations the highest abundance.

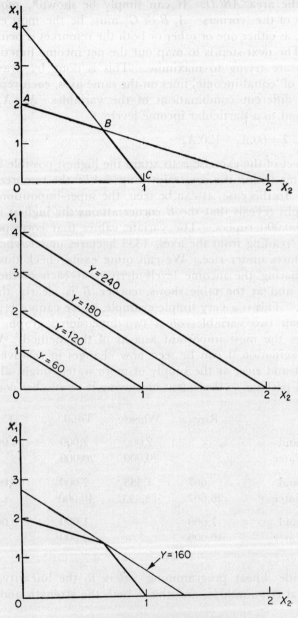

Fig. 8: Linear Programming

within the area $ABCO$. It can simply be shown*, moreover, that one of the 'corners' (A, B or C) must be the most efficient solution, as either one or other or both the resources is being fully used. The next step is to map out the net income function (Y) that we are trying to maximise. This is done by drawing a number of 'equal-income' lines on the same axes, each representing the different combinations of the variables (X_1, X_2) that correspond to a particular income level:

$$Y = 60.X_1 + 120.X_2$$

The object of the exercise is to attain the highest possible level of net income within the constraints imposed by the resource availability. In this case, as can be seen, the super-imposition of the two graphs reveals that the B corner attains the highest income level: 160,000 rupees. The variate values that correspond to this are (reading from the axes) 1333 hectares under wheat and 667 hectares under rice. We can quite easily check this result by comparing the income levels derived at each of the three corners, and as the table shows, corner B is clearly the best solution. This is a very simple example, as we cannot represent more than two variables on a two-dimensional graph, but it illustrates the most important aspects of the method. With a little imagination it can be seen how changes in relative prices of wheat and rice, or the supply of more water, might alter the solution, perhaps to the extent of moving it to another corner.

		Rice	Wheat	Total	Y
$A:$	Land	—	2,000	2,000	120,000
	Water	—	20,000	20,000	
$B:$	Land	667	1,333	2,000	160,000
	Water	26,667	13,333	40,000	
$C:$	Land	1,000	—	1,000	120,000
	Water	40,000	—	40,000	

The title 'linear programming' refers to the linearity of the functional relationships, and this is both the strength and weak-

*See the excellent exposition in Baumol (1965).

ness of the method. The strength lies in the simplicity of the computation, which allows very large problems to be handled rapidly, albeit by computer. The weakness of the method is this linearity – it cannot take into account precisely those economies of scale and discontinuities that are central to the development process. None the less, apart from the application to agriculture, where linear programming is widely applied to problems of farm management, there are two other applications of particular interest. The first is multi-product process industries such as chemicals and oil refining, where a varied range of products are obtained from a common feedstock and produced within the bounds of plant capacity at different stages. This gives a linear model which will rapidly produce the optimal 'output mix' in response to variations in demand and prices from one week to the next. The second is the well-known 'transport problem' mentioned above, where the linearity in costs between any two points (i.e. unit cost per ton-kilometre multiplied by the distance) is suitable for linear programming and a very large number of different routes may be examined. In principle the input–output matrix of Chapter 9 is also linear in form, but the difficulty of precisely defining the capacity constraints at a sectoral level and the reduction of the whole economy to direct proportionality mean that its optimisation is an exercise of mainly academic interest.

There do exist methods of programming that are non-linear, particularly *quadratic* and *integer* programming. The first allows for some adjustment to the fact that investment functions in particular are 'curved' as the cost of new plant does not increase proportionately with the capacity installed – rather the unit cost declines with size (Figure 9). Thus the relationship between investment costs (K) in relation to capacity (Q) is such that although

$$\frac{dK}{dQ} > 0$$

we have $\dfrac{d^2K}{dQ^2} < 0$

and thus unit costs decline with size:

$$\frac{d}{dQ}\left\{\frac{(K)}{Q}\right\} < 0$$

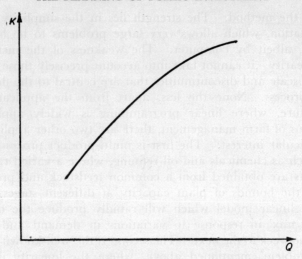

FIG. 9: Quadratic Capital Cost Function

The simplest functional form to approximate this over relevant portions of the curve, is the quadratic:*

$$K^2 = a + bQ$$

the *slope* of which is linear and problems in the maximisation of which (subject to linear constraints) are soluble by a modified form of linear programming. A variant of this is known as *separable* programming, where the curve is divided into a number of linear segments, each of which can be examined with linear-programming method until a more precise 'solution area' is found and the segments progressively reduced in size until a precise solution is found.

Where the relationship between capacity and capital cost is *integral* (that is, that there are actual 'steps' in capacity rather than infinite gradation in plant size – see Figure 10) then the method of *integer programming* is applied. This is a time-consuming procedure, requiring the use of very fast and large computers, as in principle all alternatives have to be examined because the 'corners' and 'slopes' of linear programming do not exist. Moreover, the number of possible combinations in any real

*That is: $K = \sqrt{a + bQ}$

problem is normally so large* that some method of simplification on the basis of linear programming is usually employed to find an approximate solution, and then the integral alternatives around that point examined individually to find the one with the greatest NPV.

Non-linearity in unit investment costs *and* integrality may well turn up together where not only is it necessary to install plant in discrete units but also larger units have lower unit costs when fully used. In consequence, the choice of optimal allocation over time or space will require a balance between excess capacity and scale economies of the type explored earlier in this chapter, although in a more complex fashion. Model building has evolved in this direction in recent years, combining elements of dynamic and spatial analysis, non-linear programming and multi-product planning: the particular problem being the conflict between economies of scale on the one hand and the costs of excess capacity and transport from plant to market on the other.

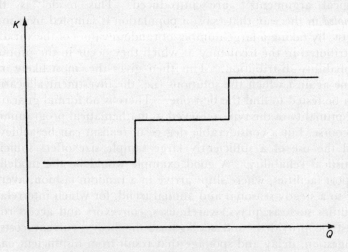

FIG. 10: Integer Capital Cost Function

*Suppose that there are five alternative plant sizes and ten possible locations, then optimal allocation would mean examining about forty billion separate allocations, each with its costs and benefits to be calculated.

Specifically, such models have been evolved* for the chemical industry in India and electric power generation in Mexico, both countries with a federal structure and ambitious industrialisation strategies.

Further Points

These modelling methods, then, are a considerable aid to investment allocation, but to the extent that they become more complex in order to approximate to the nature of the real world they become intractable to even the most powerful computer. This is further complicated when, along the lines discussed in Chapter 7, probability distributions are introduced in place of single variate values. It then becomes virtually impossible to explore all the possible combinations of variable values (and thus project results and programme valuations) and *simulation* methods have been developed to cope with the problem. Simulation involves the construction of a complex model within which ranges of parameter variables, multiple constraints, indivisibilities and 'logical arguments'† are introduced. This model is then *sampled* in the way that (say) a population is sampled by a sociologist, by taking a large number of random values of the variables distributed in the frequency at which they occur in the proposed probability distribution. This then gives the 'most likely' outcome against which the solutions (i.e. the investment allocation) can be tested to find the best one. There is no formal guarantee of optimality of the type achieved in mathematical programming, of course, but a considerable degree of realism can be achieved, and the use of a sufficiently large sample size offers sufficient statistical reliability. A good example would be the modelling of port facilities, where ships arrive in a random fashion, averaging to a steady seasonal and annual trend, for which interrelated facilities such as quays, warehouses, conveyors and access roads must be provided, and set against the heavy current costs of congestion, delay and spoilage that result from insufficient capacity. Alternative arrival patterns are generated in proportion to their frequency in the past, adjusted for overall traffic growth, and the costs and benefits of a limited number of possible port

---

*See Manne (1967) and Goreux and Manne (1973) respectively.
†E.g. of the form 'if A then B'.

expansion plans compared for each one. The plan that, on average, results in the highest NPV (or lowest total cost) is then chosen, as it maximises the *expected* value of port operations.

The best and most up-to-date of the modelling surveys is undoubtedly Blitzer (1975), while Manne (1967) and Goreux and Manne (1973) describe specific country applications, and Judge and Takayama (1973) contains a collection of studies in economic planning over space and time. Careful reading of these four books will give a clearer idea of what is involved than any single theoretical text. Baumol (1965) is a very good introduction to linear and non-linear programming within the context of microeconomic analysis, while Todaro (1970) illustrates the use of linear programming in the case of development planning. At the more advanced level, Sengupta and Fox (1971) explain the theory of optimisation as applied to quantitative models of economic processes, while White (1969) and Scott (1971) may be consulted on dynamic and spatial programming respectively. At a technical level, the range of applications is enormous, as the perusal of any professional journal such as the *Operations Research Quarterly* will indicate, while at a practical operational level, Barnard and Nix (1973) provide an excellent guide to the application of models to farm planning and control. None the less, it should always be remembered that mathematical models are no better than the quality of the data and assumptions as to objectives that are fed into them, and can often deceive by virtue of their apparent exactitude.

CHAPTER 11

PUBLIC INVESTMENT AND ECONOMIC STRATEGY

ALTHOUGH national economic strategy in the aggregate is not the subject of this book, it might be somewhat misleading if any discussion of these considerations were to be omitted, however brief. Within the space of a chapter we can do little more than indicate the relevant problems, and confine ourselves to those most directly connected to public investment planning. In consequence, we shall consider three specific topics: the choice of techniques, the state and foreign investment, and the decentralised planning model. Before this, so as to place them in a proper context, we must make some general observations as to the nature of the ' strategic problem ' itself. This strikes at the root of all forms of planning ' at the margin ' (as project and sectoral planning must inevitably be) because the nature of the underlying problems of underdevelopment relate to the structure of the economy itself.

The condition of most underdeveloped market economies is such as to be quite adequately defined as 'dependent dualism'. By this we mean a poor economy, within which there exists a relatively modern 'corporate' sector (composed of export enterprises, industry, large traders and the state apparatus) occupying a minority of the work-force but accounting for the greater part of national income. The majority of the population subsists from peasant agriculture and petty tertiary activities in the urban slums, but only receives a small part of national income, due to both low productivity and exploitation by the corporate sector. This dualism is based on the uneven development of capitalism in such countries and manifests itself in the relatively advanced machine-intensive *technology* of the modern sector on the one hand, and the special relationship with *foreign capital* on the other. The consequences in economic terms include the continued reliance on exported raw materials and imported equipment to sustain growth, narrow domestic markets, problems with food supply, spatial imbalance, internal migration to the cities and chronic difficulties with the balance of payments. The social structure that accompanies this economic structure (both sustaining and being sustained by it) frequently includes the penetration of the corporate sector by multi-national corporations, and the domination of the state by the rich (landlords, traders and industrialists) or by the bureaucracy itself, often with overt military support. The proletarian and commercial-farmer groups are, by the nature of limited economic development, relatively small and may well have a greater affinity of interest with these élites than with the 'excluded though exploited' masses in the countryside and slums, lending stability to the social structure.

It is within this widespread type of economic and social structure, which appears to be endemic to mixed economies on the periphery of the international market system, and which we are calling 'dependent dualism', that questions of public economic strategy must be considered. This raises wide issues which penetrate to the very core of political economy, particularly the basis of political support for the state, and which logically return us to the problem of the validity of the assumption that the public sector is operated so as to achieve economic development (which we mentioned at the outset of this book) as well as specific questions such as income redistribution that we have encountered. Two aspects of the economic role of the state in the dependent dual economy that have not been touched upon so far in our exposition are strategy with respect to technology and to foreign capital. These are vital topics precisely because they characterise the relationship* between the modern corporate sector of the underdeveloped economy and the international capitalist system, a relationship which has probably generated and certainly main-

---

*Paralleled by particular political relationships between the central capitalist powers and the domestic elite on the one hand, and between the latter and popular movements on the other.

tains the dependency and dualism towards the reduction of which we have so far assumed economic strategy to be directed. Specifically, this involves the discussion of the 'choice of technique' in public investment planning and of the involvement of foreign capital in state projects.

A separate aspect of public investment planning, but one which also bears upon the nature of state intervention in the economy, is that of the feasibility of decentralising investment decisions. In undertaking project appraisal and microplanning to the depth suggested in this book, a development administration is decentralising its planning as far as the unit of analysis is concerned, but the centre of decision presumably remains with central government. However, the prospect of devolving the investment decision to agencies 'in the field' offers considerable attraction in terms of both executive efficiency and ' democratisation ' of administration itself.

Public Investment and the Choice of Technique

Our first topic is that of the 'choice of technique', sometimes known as the problem of 'appropriate technology'. The relevant point here is that different techniques of production involve different proportions of inputs to produce the same output, and thus for a given output pattern there is a 'best' input combination to be chosen. The particular form that this problem takes in the context of underdevelopment is the commonly observed phenomenon of a coexistent shortage of capital* and a surplus of labour, but a simultaneous use of an ' inappropriate ' capital-intensive and labour-saving technology (usually of a type used in developed economies), particularly in industry. Specifically, manufacturing may account for 25 per cent of GDP but only 15 per cent of the national work-force, and while output is itself growing at 10 per cent a year, the work-force might well expand at only 5 per cent, so that the distortion gets steadily worse. The consequences for both resource utilisation and income distribution are clearly serious, because these 'modern' techniques of production involve substantial proportions if imported inputs (with consequent strain on the balance of payments) and limited

*We have already discussed the problem of defining 'capital' in Chapter 5.

employment potential, leading to limited redistribution of income through wages.

The orthodox analysis of this contradiction of the use of capital-intensive production techniques in a labour-surplus economy is quite simply set up on the basis of the assumption that there exist alternative combinations of capital (K) and labour (L) that can produce a given output (X), and that firms choose the minimum-cost combination of inputs ('technique') on the basis of the relative cost of capital, as represented by the interest rate (r), and of labour, as represented by the wage (w). The firm is then supposed to choose the technique (i.e. combination of capital and labour) that minimises costs, which will correspond to the point where the slope of the cost-line (C) is the same as that of the technical-substitution curve (F), as shown in Figure 11.* Further, on a macroeconomic level, if there is a shortage of capital and surplus of labour, then the wage rate relative to the interest rate would be forced down on a free market, and the firm would logically move towards more labour-intensive techniques (i.e. 'down along the F-curve') until in aggregate a balance is achieved with full utilisation of both resources.

The evident failure of techniques to be chosen in a manner such as to adjust to the factor availability in an underdeveloped economy evokes three responses, corresponding to the main axioms of the argument. *First* it can be argued that factor prices are not free to move, and in particular that wage rates are held above

*This is simply shown algebraically and formally. The object is to minimise costs:

$$C=rK+wL$$

the two inputs being related through the production function:

$$X=F(K, L)$$

The solution is found where

$$dC=r.dK+w.dL=0$$

or $$\frac{r}{w} = \frac{dK}{dL} = F'$$

That is, where the ratio of input prices (r/w) is equal to the slope of the technical substitution curve (F').

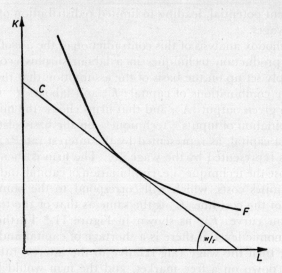

Fig. 11: Choice of Technique

the market equilibrium rate by trades unions and social legislation while capital costs are held down by cheap finance for state banks and tax incentives. The logical response is to suggest that wages rates be cut or capital charges raised, and at the very least to apply appropriate shadow prices in the public sector. *Second* it can be argued that the *F*-curve is not in fact continuous, and that in practice only the traditional labour-intensive but inefficient techniques and the modern, capital-intensive but efficient techniques are available: with only these two extremes to choose between, the latter is naturally chosen. The logical response here is to devise techniques that are 'intermediate' between the two extremes by undertaking specific research programmes; this is the basis of the 'intermediate technology movement'. *Third*, it can be argued that the product type itself often varies with the input combination used, and that (say) a factory-made cloth is qualitatively different from the effort of the artisan. This is as much a problem of 'taste' as of anything else, the impact of advertising and the impact of foreign cultures biasing consumer tastes towards 'modern' products. Here the logical response is to attempt to stimulate support for national culture and 'simpler' consumer goods, modes of transport and so on.

All these arguments have some truth to them, but if we refer back to the analysis sketched at the beginning of this chapter, it would appear that both the orthodox analysis and its modifications miss the point. In fact, the 'wrong' choice of technique is indeed wrong as far as the disadvantaged masses are concerned, but it is 'right' for the owners, administrators and existing employees of the corporate sector. For them, capital-intensive techniques mean high profits and wage rates, a secure place for the technician and above all a continued need for the services of the foreign corporation. The concentration of income and power in the hands of a fraction of the population leads, moreover, to a demand for the 'luxury' products such as cars and televisions, which can only be produced by using foreign technology and capital-intensive methods. The real issue, then, is not the simple one of cost-minimisation and equilibrium in input markets, but rather a question of the *style* of development and the resulting socio-economic structure. 'Dependent dualism' only requires that there be high rates of accumulation and growth in the *corporate* sector in order to be successful *in its own terms*, it does not require that there be growth in peasant incomes or urban employment – so there is no particular logic in choosing labour-intensive techniques of production when development of the *whole* economy is not really the aim, particularly since this would probably mean the massive shift of resources away from the corporate sector and a severe reduction in the links with foreign enterprise.

Public Investment and Foreign Capital

Our second topic is the relationship between the state and foreign capital. This is of particular relevance to the 'dependent' nature of Third World economies. By this term we mean the situation in which a substantial proportion of the decisions as to production and accumulation are made outside the economy itself, normally through the agency of foreign enterprises now that direct colonialism is uncommon. This is part of the process by which, on the one hand, the dependent economy is 'locked' into the world economy as a supplier of raw materials against imported capital goods and technology (generally at disadvantageous terms) and by which, on the other hand, foreign companies may control large portions of domestic resource extraction, industry and finance*. In this context, the relationship between the public sector and foreign capital, in the form of either official finance or joint ventures, will have a strategic dimension beyond the immediate costs and benefits involved.

Due to the exigencies of public finance† in most developing countries, which lead to shortages of capital funds, as well as the chronic lack of foreign exchange as they attempt to accelerate growth, external financial assistance is an attractive source of both. This may take the form of gifts and concessionary loans from individual governments, soft loans from multilateral institutions such as the World Bank, and loans at market rates from international commercial banks. Much of this finance involves a substantial 'grant element' and despite the problems inherent in 'tied aid' (which obliges the recipient to buy equipment from one country and thus perhaps exclude lower cost alternative suppliers), in itself it undoubtedly represents a net gain to the economy, particularly if the recipient government has properly determined the projects to receive foreign finance. Of course, if foreign finance is accepted on an unplanned basis, a large number of uncoordinated and capital-intensive projects may be undertaken merely because 'aid' is available. However, the real problem arises from the very large external debts built up by many poor countries, the total of which quite frequently exceeds a sum more than double the annual export income, the repayments on which can take up more than a quarter of that income each year. This burden is, none the less, equivalent to the transfer of foreign exchange expenditure on imports through time, to the benefit of the economy. The real cost is the consequences of exposure of the government to the 'leverage' of international capital (frequently under the 'chairmanship' of the

---

*This does not necessarily mean majority ownership of the shares in a local company, as control can be exercised through nominees, franchises and specialised inputs. Indeed most multinationals now exercise control through technology rather than shareholding in any case.

†Except for the oil producers, tax income cannot usually be raised much above current government expenditure (itself pushed upwards by the pressure for greater military and social welfare expenditure), nor can large public enterprise profits be made.

IBRD and IMF), which can result in the rescheduling of existing debt, or new lending being withheld from governments attempting to implement radical land reforms or reduce foreign control over industry. The cost, therefore, of foreign finance may well be reflected in the restriction of strategic choice to continuation of dependent dualism.

Although the state can borrow abroad as an independent agent, in order to obtain foreign technology a 'joint venture' with a transnational corporation may be the only alternative to direct penetration of a strategic branch by the foreign company, because technology cannot be purchased as such. It does permit planning control over investment and production, absorption of the technology by local technicians and participation in the profits, but from the point of view of the foreign corporations the political protection and finance provided by the state are considerable advantages too, and in any case they are accustomed to minority ownership and the extraction of profits through other mechanisms such as transfer pricing* and management contracts.

As a result of the interaction of those two influences, even though the state may have intervened in the economy in order to support or even replace domestic enterprise against the inroads of the multinationals, it often finds itself in a close interrelationship with them. This, in turn, means that the scope for the use of labour-intensive techniques, or the implementation of ownership changes, or the extension of state control over the economy, or the achievement of substantial income-redistributive reforms is necessarily limited, not only by direct external 'leverage' but by the technocratic nature of the public administration itself. In consequence, it is not surprising that the full-scale introduction of (say) income weights or even of integrated development planning itself is still far from common in non-socialist economies.

Decentralised Planning of Public Investment

The process of project appraisal on a marginal basis as an administrative process has led to the exploration of models of an economy where ownership of enterprises is decentralised (i.e.

---

*By which, say, a local affiliate of an international car firm would pay excessively high prices for engines imported from its sister company in the mother country, and thus transfer profits to the latter.

vested in the work-force at the plant level) within a centrally planned economy. The theory rests on the supposition that the enterprises maximise value-added (i.e. profits plus wages), but that the control of input and output prices remains with the central planning office. By manipulating these prices, output from the branches can be stimulated and the input mix varied, while retaining the incentives to efficiency in the individual enterprise. This also has attractions in terms of local 'freedom' in contrast to the *dirigisme* of conventional central planning.

Such models start by looking at the economy (or the sectors to be planned in this way) from the centre. There is an objective function ($\mathcal{Z}$) to be maximised (net economic output, or value added) subject to a total budget constraint ($\overline{K}$), by allocating capital (K_i) to each branch (i) so as to produce discounted income (B_i) net of discounted operating costs. Formally, then, we must

$$\text{maximise } \mathcal{Z} = \sum_i (B_i - K_i) \qquad \begin{array}{l} \text{for } i = 1 \ldots n \\ \text{subject to } \sum_i K_i \leqslant \overline{K} \end{array}$$

the solution being found by maximising the single 'Lagrangian function'*

$$L = \mathcal{Z} + \lambda(\overline{K} - \Sigma K_i)$$

where the parameter (λ) is known as the 'Lagrange Multiplier'. The conditions for the maximum† are then

$$\frac{dB_i}{dK_i} = 1 + \lambda$$

$$\Sigma \overline{K}_i = \overline{K}$$

In other words, when the investment budged ($\overline{K}$) is fully used, then the marginal value of investment funds (λ) is the return on investment in the marginal project.

*For a good explanation of this, see Baumol (1965).

†An extremum, actually, and the full Kuhn-Tucker conditions are

$$\frac{dL}{dK_i} = \frac{dB_i}{dK_i} - 1 - \lambda \leqslant 0 \quad (\text{if} \neq 0, \ K_i = 0)$$

$$\frac{dL}{d\lambda} = -\Sigma K_i + \overline{K} \geqslant 0 \quad (\text{if} \neq 0, \ \lambda = 0)$$

We now turn to the individual enterprises, each of which tries to maximise its own surplus (Y_j)

$$Y_j = B_j - \pi K_j$$

in terms of the net discounted income (B_j), the capital funds obtained from the centre (K_j) and the price paid for them (π). The maximisation of the objective by each enterprise means that

$$\frac{dB_j}{dK_j} = \pi \quad \text{for } j = 1 \ldots n$$

Clearly, then, if the central planning authority (with the central bank) charges the enterprises a price which will balance the sum of all the requests from the enterprises for funds (ΣK_j) against the available budget ($\bar{K}$), this is equivalent to setting

$$\pi = 1 + \lambda$$

so that the result of the combined surplus-maximising efforts of the enterprises is formally the same as the maximisation of the total surplus from the centre.

This principle can be applied to the other inputs (such as foreign exchange) or centrally purchased products, so as to evolve an optimum solution with respect to the allocation of resources, within a context where the income-maximising effort of individual enterprises is preserved. As such, it has formed the basis of justifications of the decentralised cooperative economy of the 'Yugoslav' type and the tentative move towards decision making at the enterprise level in Russia. Leaving aside the social implications, such as the emergence of income differentials between workers in one branch against those in another, the model depends on the crucial assumption that all the costs and benefits of the expansion of a particular branch can be reflected through the administered price system into the 'enterprise accounts', so that a 'social market economy' can be achieved.

This assumption is the crucial drawback in the context of development planning, where almost by definition there exist severe distortions in the *existing* economic structure which require the application of severe 'jumps' administered from the centre. In specific terms, we could mention the surplus labour problem as an instance of this difficulty, where although the shadow price for labour* might be near to zero, this could not be the wage rate. Again, the process of planned industrial integration cannot be represented in terms of benefits to individual enterprises, as we have seen in Chapter 8. To put it the other way round, such a model can only operate *within* a given economic structure, and cannot be used to change it, although it might well be highly desirable after such necessary changes have been effected.

Further Points

The theme that has run throughout this chapter bears repetition precisely because it does tend to get neglected in the enthusiasm for method and technique, a neglect which may be sustained by the unwillingness of the influential 'aid' institutions to comment publicly upon strategic issues.† We have seen that the appraisal of two apparently technical problems (the choice of technique and the evaluation of foreign investment) do in fact raise severe issues of economic development, and perhaps *the* strategic problem: the style of this development in relation to the problem of dependent dualism. Similarly, the attractions (in terms of both economic efficiency and local independence) of decentralised planning are misleading unless their reliance upon a given economic and social structure is recognised. Thus, once again, we return to the need for an approach to microplanning that is integrated to the national plan.

On the broad analysis of underdevelopment presented in this chapter, the best book is probably still Baran (1957), although Barrett-Brown (1974) is also very useful, while Leys (1975) and Furtado (1970) give important case studies. The orthodox view, in contrast, is presented in any standard text such as Kindleberger (1965). The essay by Bell included in Chenery (1974) is a thoughtful discussion of the political constraints upon the state engaged upon reform of economic structures. Probably the best-known work on the choice of technique is Sen (1968), but a large number of authors have addressed themselves to the problem in the context of surplus labour – from Lewis (1954) to Little and Mirrlees (1974).

*Which would have to be applied to the enterprises so that they would make decisions on the basis of the true opportunity cost of labour.

†Or perhaps, indeed, to reveal their own true priorities.

The well-known ILO 'surveys' of employment in a number of countries (including Colombia, Philippines, Kenya and Sri Lanka) contain useful practical material on this topic too. On the transfer of technology, Vaitsos (1974) is very informative and clear, while Schumacher (1973) himself leads the intermediate technology 'movement', although Bhalla (1975) does show that a wide variety of alternative techniques are available already in a number of manufacturing branches. Chenery (1974) contains a good analysis of the impact of the choice of technique upon income distribution. The literature on direct foreign investment is enormous, and from all shades of opinion, but in the specific context of this chapter a good statement of the 'orthodox' position on aid and investment flows is given by Pearson (1969), while a brief but clear analysis of the technical arguments is given by Healy (1971), and the political implications of external indebtedness are excellently treated in Payer (1974). Reading on joint ventures is unfortunately scarce, but Radice (1975) may be found useful on multinationals, and Lal (1975) looks at the cost–benefit analysis of private foreign investment in developing countries, while Johnson (1975) presents the 'case for the defence' in a lucid manner. Finally, on decentralised planning, the seminal work is undoubtedly Lerner (1944), while the pure theory is well developed in Marglin (1963) and Qayum (1963), and its introduction to the Russian planning system is described in Ellman (1971). The advantages of a decentralised worker-managed economy are enthusiastically propounded by Vaneck (1970).

CLOSING REMARKS

We have now reached the close of this brief exposition of public investment planning method, an exposition based more upon the needs of teaching and professional practice than on theoretical elegance. It contains, therefore, hostages to fortune in the form of inconsistencies and unresolved questions. None the less, this risk is worthwhile if the informal style is also a more helpful one, and in any case it reflects the nature of the topic itself.

In this second part of the book we have examined the various methods by which the project–analysis aspect of public investment programming can be integrated to the national planning process. We have explored a somewhat heterogeneous collection of such methods, ranging from the simple materials balance to the complexities of dynamic allocation models. The main effect of these is to allow the lacunae in project planning observed in Part I to be filled. The particular gaps in the conventional exposition of project appraisal that appeared to be the most important were the determination of the planning discount rate, the relationship between production branches, and the search for optimal investment patterns. The exploration of the methods needed to resolve these problems required explicit statements as to overall economic strategy, which were only apparently avoided by modern project appraisal methodologies. Indeed, it was suggested that the analysis of two specific topics (choice of technique and foreign aid) can be positively misleading if this is not done. In consequence, a greater amount of 'political economy' than is conventional in this field has been introduced to the text: although this might seem to reduce the 'objectivity' of the methodology, it is just this supposed characteristic that can be misleading insofar as it offers a temptation to ignore the wider issues of underdevelopment.

This last point deserves further comment precisely because it may well be that much of the potential of project analysis lies in its *heuristic* value. In other words, the analytical procedure forces our attention upon development problems far beyond a particular investment decision, and obliges us to make concrete statements about the economic structure of a country, its dynamics, and the precise meaning of development strategies. For example, having worked through the numerical problem on mechanisation in agriculture supplied on p. 156, the student is in a better position to grasp the contradictions of the so-called Green Revolution, while the economist or engineer who has worked through a location study for a cement plant will have a much better idea of what is involved in a term such as 'spatial balance'.

This heuristic value is not confined to the lecture hall, then, rather the opposite. The process of public investment planning, if carried out in a rational manner, requires that the planners themselves translate the broad declarations and ambitions of the national plan into practical actions within a determinate socioeconomic structure. Indeed, it might well be argued that the contents of this book are best taught not at the university but rather within the planning organisation itself, so that they can be seen within a specific economic and administrative context.

PART III

SUPPLEMENTARY MATERIAL

THIS final section of the book contains supplementary material that may be found useful by teachers and students. It is, in fact, itself a selection from the range of material used on the Cambridge Development Course in recent years. The section containing 'numerical problems' and 'essay topics' is suitable for students to use in their own time, as it consists of a selection from recent examination questions for the Diploma in Development and the Diploma in Development Economics. The kind permission of the Cambridge University Examinations Board to publish these is gratefully acknowledged. Originally the numerical problems were intended to take just over an hour to complete, and the essay topics about three-quarters of an hour, although the latter could clearly be used as the basis of more extensive compositions. The 'workshop exercise' is a much longer affair, involving group participation, and some suggestions for its implementation are given at the appropriate point. A set of 'discount tables' has been included because, although they are very widely used professionally, they are often surprisingly hard to come by separately and cheaply. Finally, the full bibliography referred to in the text is listed: here an attempt has been made to refer only to published books and articles readily available to a university or planning office library. Indeed, in combination with a collection covering the relevant economic, social and physical characteristics of the economy or sector in question, this list might well provide the basis for a working library in such institutions.

NUMERICAL PROBLEMS AND ESSAY TOPICS

Numerical Problems
(1) Next year it is proposed to upgrade a road carrying heavy port traffic so as to reduce transport costs. The capital cost of the improvement would be 20 million pesos, saving 10 pesos on every vehicle

movement. It is estimated that traffic volume (which will be un-affected by the improvement) will reach some 300,000 movements/annum next year, increasing thereafter by 20,000 movements per annum. The 'planning horizon' for this project is fifteen years, and the residual value of the investment may be taken as one-quarter of the original cost.

First, calculate the net present value of the project using the data given. *Second*, what would the NPV be if there were no traffic growth at all from next year? What, roughly, would the annual traffic growth have to be in order to justify the expansion? *Third*, the Ministry of Transport calculates that the cost composition of the two items is as follows:

	Capital cost	Vehicle savings
Local materials	60%	20%
Foreign exchange	10%	70%
Labour	30%	10%
	100%	100%

Also the Planning Commission estimates that the opportunity cost of foreign exchange is 20% above its market price, and that of labour is 50% of its market price. Recalculate the NPV of the project under these assumptions. *Fourth*, what conclusions would you draw from these calculations?

(2) Arcadia is embarking upon an electrification programme, and must choose between thermal or hydroelectric generation schemes in order to expand the system by 100 MW over the next twenty years. Thermal sets of 50 MW could be installed in the port city, coming on stream next year and in ten years' time – each taking one year to build – but having to be replaced after 10 years of operation, with no scrap value. A hydroelectric barrage of 100 MW capacity could be installed in the mountains, also taking one year to build and having a life of 40 years.

The cost of construction and operations are shown below; the total operating costs over the life of the plant have already been discounted to the first year of operation at 10%

	Costs (million florins) of:	
	Construction	Operations
Thermal Plant (each)	500	1000
Hydroelectric Plant	3000	500

We have the following breakdown of costs provided by the consulting engineers:

		Construction		Operations	
		Hydro	Thermal	Hydro	Thermal
Labour:	skilled	10%	10%	30%	10%
	unskilled	30%	10%	20%	—
Materials:	imported	20%	50%	10%	80%
	local	40%	30%	40%	10%
	Total	100%	100%	100%	100%

The Planning Commission has indicated that the following data are to be applied:

(a) Discount Rate is 10%

(b) Shadow Wage Rate for unskilled labour is 30% of the market wage.

(c) The Opportunity Cost of local materials is 80% of the market price.

Given this information, stating clearly any other assumptions you may wish to make, follow these steps:

(i) calculate the construction and operating costs in terms of shadow prices;

(ii) lay out the relevant costs over time for the two schemes, over the life of the hydroelectric project;

(iii) find the net present cost of the two alternatives;

(iv) on the basis of this appraisal, indicate which is the best choice.

Now consider the direction of the effects of the following changes upon your choice:

(a) a higher cost of fuel oil,

(b) a higher rate of discount,

(c) a lower shadow wage rate,

(d) a lower rate of growth of energy requirements.

(3) It is proposed that four teams of bullocks working on a 200-hectare farm be replaced by a tractor. This will involve an increase in the yield of wheat on the land from 1 to 2 tons a hectare, but also increased costs of fertilizer and fuel for the tractor. These increases are equivalent

to 25 Rupees per hectare, but there will be a saving of 20 Rupees per hectare in labour costs and the extra yield, which with wheat at 40 Rupees a ton is considerable. Suppose that the tractor costs the farmer 30,000 Rupees (but he can get credit from the Agricultural Development Bank at 5% over 7 years – the life of the tractor) and that he can sell the bullock teams for 1,250 Rupees each, then work out the annual value of the change to him. Then, allowing for the fact that rural labour has a zero opportunity cost to the economy and the planning discount rate is 10%, work out the annual value of this mechanization to the economy as a whole.

Using your results, and assuming them to be representative of farm mechanization in the region (which has about a million hectares under wheat) where a bullock team provides employment for two men a hundred days a year – work out the effects on output and employment of complete mechanization. What implications does your answer have in the context of the success (or otherwise) of the so-called 'Green Revolution'?

(4) A decision must be made as to cement plant expansion to meet requirements for the next decade. These are estimated at 300,000 tons per annum for the five years 1979–83 and 500,000 per annum for the years 1984–8. A choice must be made between building a 500,000-ton-capacity plant in 1978, or one of 300,000 in 1978 and expansion by 200,000 tons in 1983. The relevant costs are shown below.

Analyse the two possible plans over the 1978–88 period, allowing a direct proportion of the original capital cost for scrap value – you may take all equipment life as 15 years. The relevant rate of interest for public loans to state enterprise is 5%, but the Planning Commission believe that 12% would better reflect the 'opportunity cost of capital'. What action should be taken? How would this be influenced by (a) a higher growth in demand, (b) uncertainty as to future requirements? Which other factors might the Planning Commission wish to take into account before making a recommendation and how might these affect the initial result?

	Capacity ('000 tons)		
	500	300	200
Capital cost ($ mn)	24	18	12
Overheads ($ mn/annum)	2.00	1.30	0.90
Operating costs ($/ton)	10	11	12

(5) A recent ILO mission studied the choice of technique for sealing cans, and collected the following data on the two possible choices.

	Initial cost of machinery	Life of machinery (years)	Cost of factory space	Workers per machine	Monthly wage	Rate of output (cans per min.)
Technique				(1 skilled technician	@ £32.5	270
Automated	£8,000	15	£50	2(1 semiskilled	@ £20	
Semi-				(0.3 supervisor	@ £25 ea.	38
automated	£500	10	£30	1.3(1.0 unskilled	@ £17.5	

The mission collected the following data for the economy:

Average tariff on consumer imports	20%
Average tariff on capital imports	5%
Average gross return on private investment in the manufacturing sector	15%

The available information on wages is summarised:

Average[1] incomes of selected groups in rural and urban areas, 1969 (£ per annum):

	Adults	Men	Women
Rural:			
Wage employment[2]			
Large farms	68	73	46
Small farms	38	41	34
Non-agricultural enterprises	45	47	34
Self-employment			
Smallholders	113	..	..
Owners of non-agricultural enterprises	130	..	..
Urban:			
Wage employment[2]			
Formal sector	443	471	297
Statutory minimum wage in the formal sector	..	106	84
Informal urban	40	..	..
Self-employment			
Informal urban	60	..	..

.. =Not available

[1] There are often wide variations in earnings around the averages shown. This applies particularly to smallholders.

[2] Regular employees.

The automated technique is not divisible and has a potential weekly output of 600,000 cans per week. The semi-automated technique is divisible. Current demand is 350,000 cans per week. Material and other costs are small, and virtually the same for both techniques.

(a) which process would you expect to be chosen at current market prices?

(b) which process appears on the present evidence socially preferable?

(c) what additional information would you request in preparing your evaluation, how might it be collected, and how would you use it?

(6) Country X's foreign-exchange reserves stand at US $7.5 billion, and its outstanding foreign debt is negligible. More than 90% of the value of its exports is generated by a single commodity – a non-renewable natural resource – whose international price, successfully doubled last year, is maintained by the restrictions on export supplies operated by a 10-country group of which X is a member. X's quota under this arrangement is 7% of total group exports; and at current prices and marketing policies this should yield annual export receipts of US $5.5 billion to X from the commodity (representing some 30% of G.D.P.).

Estimates of X's reserves of the commodity range from less than 10 years' further extraction at current rates to as much as 30 years or more. The growth in the volume of world demand for the commodity over the next decade is also uncertain – because of worldwide economic instability, imperfect information on the investments undertaken in substitutes, and the possibility of new uses for the commodity in question – and estimates of the average annual growth rate range from 2 to 10%. At least two other countries of X's importance as producers of the commodity do not belong to the group enforcing quotas, while some of its members are known to be quite anxious to increase the volume of their exports.

X is also endowed with substantial unexploited deposits of iron ore and coal, together with extensive hydroelectric possibilities. Consequently the government have decided to go ahead with a large-scale steel project, whose forecasts include the following features:

EXPECTED VALUES IN MILLIONS OF US $ AT PRESENT PRICES

Total foreign-exchange cost of plant and equipment (to be incurred in five equal and consecutive annual stages)[1]	8,500
Annual foreign-exchange cost of production (to be incurred from the fifth year)[2]	1,750
Annual production at international prices (begins in the sixth year)	5,260

[1]Excluding interest payments. N.B. Because of special conditions these costs rise by 15% to the extent that they are financed by World Bank loans.

[2]Excluding interest payments. These costs cover alloying metals, replacements and spare parts, patents and licences.

Steel exports from this project are expected to be some 95% of production from year 6 to year 10, and then progressively to decline, over the next 15 years, to an annual value of US $ 3.5 billion (at present prices) from the fifteenth year. Iron ore and coal deposits are known to be sufficient for at least 50 years; but it is not intended to export these resources unprocessed.

The steel project could be financed in a combination of one or more of the following ways: (i) by varying the rate of extraction of the main export commodity; (ii) by using foreign exchange reserves; (iii) by taking US dollar loans from the World Bank; and (iv) by taking US dollar loans from a syndicate of Euro-market banks. World Bank loans would be at $8\frac{1}{2}\%$ interest per annum; for 20 years; with an initial grace period of 5 years during which only the interest would be payable, and after which the principal would become payable in 15 equal annual instalments. Syndicated loans would be at a floating rate of interest set 2 percentage points above the 3-month London inter-bank offered (LIBO) rate on US dollars, for 12 years; with an initial grace period of 6 years during which only the interest would be payable, and after which the principal would become payable in 6 equal annual instalments.

It may be assumed that World Bank and syndicated loans can be combined; and that loans need only be taken up as successive stages of the project require finance. It may also be assumed that X's foreign-exchange reserves earn interest at the LIBO rate. (This rate now stands at 6%, but it has varied between 5 and 14% over the past 5 years.)

You are asked to advise the government of X on how to finance the foreign-exchange costs of the steel project. Describe and justify the form which your advice would take, carefully explaining any additional assumptions which you feel you have to make.

Essay Topics

(1) 'Oil in the ground is better than money in the bank' (Sheikh Yamani). Discuss in relation to the concept of optimal production patterns over time.

(2) 'If the projects are right then the aggregate economic planning is superfluous; if projects are wrong, then it is meaningless.' Discuss.

(3) Explain exactly what is implied by the use of international prices in the 'OECD' or 'Little–Mirrlees' method of calculating shadow prices. Does this method imply that world markets are 'fair'?

(4) Two alternative sources of tied foreign finance for a project are Italy and Canada. The Italians offer a loan at 5% repayable over 10 years, and the Canadians one at 2% repayable over 5 years. Which would you accept, given a planning discount rate of 10%? Would your decision be the same if the prices for Italian equipment were 20% above those of the Canadians? All calculations must be shown.

(5) It is often suggested by economists that labour-intensive methods should be used in roadworks, but engineers usually argue that the quality of mechanized methods is such that they are cheaper in the long run, as less maintenance is required and vehicle operating costs are lower. Suggest how this argument might be resolved in quantitative terms for a particular case.

(6) It has now become almost orthodox to recommend that 'income distribution weights' be used in project evaluation. Indicate how these might be integrated into the cost–benefit calculations, and discuss the implications of their use for government policy as a whole.

(7) Discuss the methods that might be used to forecast the demand for a product and market of your choice. Pay attention to data sources as well as methodology, and indicate how you would allow for the inevitable degree of uncertainty in your forecast.

(8) 'Labour-intensive construction methods are necessary in order to provide employment, redistribute income, and save scarce foreign

exchange.' 'Labour-intensive methods are inefficient, and by increasing consumption and reducing saving, they slow economic growth.' Discuss the validity of these two opinions in the context of the calculation of a shadow wage rate for use on public works.

(9) Improved income distribution is the professed aim of many governments. Suggest how such objectives might be translated into specific criteria for public sector planning purposes. Discuss the condition upon which the success of your proposal would depend.

(10) 'As a result of market distortions, capital is too cheap and labour is too expensive in the third world, so that for better resource allocation the wage rate should be lowered.' Discuss this view.

(11) The 'Little–Mirrlees' method of shadow pricing divides commodities between 'traded' and 'non-traded'. Distinguish between them, and discuss the difficulties in valuation of a non-traded good as output. What implications do your conclusions have for the method as a whole?

(12) In response to a request from your government, both France and Germany are prepared to supply agricultural machinery under 'aid' agreements. The French prices are higher than the German ones. What additional information would you require, and how would you use it, to reach a decision on a financial basis?

(13) Discuss the problems involved in the measurement of the benefits of a major road project.

(14) Define precisely what you understand by 'externalities' in project appraisal. Explain how you would measure these effects in practice, illustrating your answer by reference to at least two production sectors.

(15) The 'intersectoral integration of industry' is a basic objective in many development strategies. Explain what is meant by this concept and show how the input–output table can be used in planning at the sectoral level.

(16) Outline how you would estimate the shadow price of cement in each of the following four cases:

  (i)   Where cement is a traded input to a project;
  (ii)   Where cement is a non-traded input to a project;
  (iii) Where cement is the traded output of a project;
  (iv)   Where cement is the non-traded output of a project.

(17) Explain clearly how you would estimate the shadow wage rate for unskilled labour in (a) a rural road construction scheme and (b) an urban factory project. Refer to the data sources in your own country to illustrate your answer.

(18) The setting of the planning discount rate necessarily forms an integral part of the budgetary system, and is also related to the overall financing of the public sector. Show how different institutional structures might affect the way in which the discount rate is determined, and the implications of these for its subsequent application.

(19) Explain how you would set about evaluating a proposal from a multi-national corporation that it should exploit a mineral resource in collaboration with the public sector. Illustrate your answer with hypothetical figures.

(20) Outline the main methods used in the practice of demand forecasting, distinguishing between final and intermediate goods. In what way can the concept of uncertainty be handled within the forecasting framework?

THE ALPHA–BETA FISHERIES PROJECT*

This material* has been used by the Cambridge Course on Development for several years as the basis for a 'workshop' exercise over three days, in which the participants form fairly small 'syndicates' responsible for the analysis of the documents and the presentation of a final report on the project to the class as a whole. The following two books are recommended to the participants for general background reading before undertaking the exercise:

Mishra, S. N., and Beyer, J., *Cost–Benefit Analysis: A Case Study of the Ratnagiri Fisheries Project* (Delhi, 1976);

Digby, M., *The Organization of Fishermen's Cooperatives* (Oxford, 1973).

From: Central Planning Commission
        The Presidential Palace
        Constitution Avenue
        Metropole, Arcadia

To: Members of the Joint Committee on Special Projects

Dear Committee Member,
    A meeting of the Joint Committee on Special Projects has been convened. The project under consideration is the reorganisation of the fishing activities at the adjoining coastal villages of Alphaville and Betaville, the introduction of motor launches, the establishment of a filleting/freezing plant and the strengthening of the Cooperative.

*Jointly compiled by E. V. K. FitzGerald and A. F. Robertson.

Please find enclosed the Agenda and supporting documents. The Minister wishes me to remind you that a short report must be prepared for his decision as soon as possible after the Committee meets.

Yours sincerely,

A. Convenor
Secretary of the Committee and
Assistant to the Minister

Encs.

Joint Committee on Special Projects
The Presidential Palace
Constitution Avenue
Metropole, Arcadia

THE ALPHA–BETA FISHERIES PROJECT

The Committee is asked to consider the proposed project to re-organise the fishing activities at the neighbouring coastal villages of Alphaville and Betaville, introduce motor launches, establish a filleting/freezing plant and strengthen the NFCU Cooperative.

The Agenda for the meeting is as follows:
(1) Minutes of last meeting
(2) Discussion of IFI Report
(3) Discussion of ISS Report
(4) Discussion of specific implementation problems
(5) Drafting of report to the Minister
(6) A.O.B.

Committee members are urged to read the documents closely before the meeting.   Please find enclosed:
(1) Minutes of last meeting
(2) Suggested discussion points
(3) IFI Report
(4) ISS Report

Joint Committee on Special Projects
The Presidential Palace
Constitution Avenue
Metropole, Arcadia

Extract from:

Minutes of Last Meeting

(1) At this meeting it was decided unanimously that an economic and social feasibility study should be commissioned in order to investigate the proposed *Alpha–Beta Fisheries Project*.

(2) The neighbouring villages of Alphaville and Betaville are currently entirely engaged in inshore fishing with small craft, the catch being sun-dried and sold locally.   The income of the inhabitants is low, and the level of amenities below standard.

(3) Within the overall aims of the Special Projects (Provisions) Act of 1969, the public funding of a project of this type would be acceptable. Broadly, it was proposed that

    (*a*) the present fleet be replaced by motor launches;

    (*b*) a filleting and freezing plant be established;

    (*c*) a new quay and dredged channel be provided;

    (*d*) the road link to the main coastal highway be improved;

    (*e*) a community centre and clinic be constructed.

(4) The object would be not only to raise the incomes of the inhabitants but also to increase the spirit of entrepreneurship in the community while strengthening the local branch of the National Fishermen's Cooperative Union.

(5) It was anticipated that there might be social problems to be overcome; so that apart from determining the technical and economic feasibility of the proposal, a social survey of the community has been carried out.   In particular, it was expected that, although the greatest economic advantage would probably be obtained by rapid modernisation of the activity, this would pose social tensions that could be overcome by a slower changeover.

(6) It was decided, therefore, that the Institute of Social Studies (Metropole) be invited to prepare a report, which, with the economic report of the IFI, could form the basis of a decision by this Committee upon its next meeting.

Suggested Discussion Points

Further to Item 5 of the Agenda ('Discussion of Specific Implementation Problems') these suggestions have been supplied by the Secretariat as a guide to discussion:

(a) Is the project feasible on economic grounds ? And on these grounds, would Plan A or Plan B be preferable ? An outline of the reasons for your choice should be supplied, and the relevant calculations shown.

(b) How are traditional craft to be phased out? If Plan B is chosen, how would the (reducing) number of these remaining in the transitional years be licensed ? How should those excluded from fishing be helped ? How should ownership of the new boats be organised ? (e.g. all profits to the NFCU or leased to families ?) How would the new captains be chosen?

(c) Does the proposed scheme accord with the government's policy to eliminate poverty and distribute the benefits of development widely? Who should, and should not become members of the NFCU ? Should the scheme be administered by the Ministry of Fisheries until it is established?

(d) Balancing the economic and social implications, should the government proceed with the project? If so, which Project Plan should be adopted? Specifically, as Plan A turns out to be preferable on economic grounds, but B on social grounds, would the cost to the community of A justify the cost to the economy of B? What additional implementation measures would the Committee recommend?

Report from the International Fisheries Institute Mission

(1) *Introduction*

Following a request (TA 371/C3/63/75) under the technical assistance programme between the Arcadian Government and the International Fisheries Institute, a team of three experts (headed by Dr E. Knox) visited the area and the relevant administrative departments during January 1976. Several previous missions have looked at the problem of modernising fishing on this coast (e.g. the Stanford Research Institute in 1970, the Moscow Academy Mission in 1965 and the Imperial White Fish Authority in 1937) and so there was a considerable quantity of background information available. Recently, fishing surveys (UN/47/3001/74) of the area have been carried out by the FAO and a firm of local consulting engineers have investigated the proposed infrastructure works (Hadrian and Partners, Metropole, September 1975). The IFI team was asked to examine the economic feasibility of a plan to replace the present fleet of small fishing craft by motor launches and to freeze fish fillets instead of curing them. The following is a summary of the full report (IFI/288A/421/76) submitted to the Arcadian Government in February 1977. The monetary unit is the Arena (A), the present exchange rate being A. 15 = 1 US dollar.

The proposed project will result in the modernisation of fishing operations in the Alpha–Beta area, a substantial increase in the catch and the introduction of industry in the form of filleting and freezing processes. As a result, the community will be rapidly transformed by the new levels of income, the new organisations required, and the probable influx of workers from other areas seeking employment in secondary activities. The new forms of ownership and economic administration will strengthen and reward entrepreneurship while providing tangible evidence that enterprise is the best way of achieving material progress. In other words, the project will 'help people to help themselves'. Although the report from the ISS will deal with the social aspects of the project more fully, we would like to point out that in our considered opinion Plan A (i.e. rapid implementation) should be adopted not only because it leads to higher project benefits but also because it will make the break with traditional methods clearer and effective use of the new craft more likely – always assuming, of course, that our recommendations on previous crew training and experienced personnel are adopted. We would also suggest that private ownership of the new craft should be encouraged in order to foster entrepreneurship, and strongly urge that competitive fishing by traditional methods be prohibited, so as to prevent depletion of the fish stock.

In our opinion, then, the project is both economically and financially sound (although the exact financial structure of the eventual enterprise form has yet to be decided) and the considerable secondary employment effects anticipated will form an additional bonus. State intervention should be confined to the initial change, necessarily a mandatory one although for the community's own good, and then private enterprise be allowed to flourish.

(2) *Fishing Activities*

At present some 140 small craft, constructed from local timber and

manually propelled by three men, operate from the beaches of Alphaville and Betaville (see Institute of Social Studies Report). Catches
run at around 10 quintals (or 1000 kg) a week for each boat, equivalent
to 25 tons a year. This is sold, after drying, for A. 15/q., which provides an income of A. 150/week for each 'boat', the value being divided between proprietor and crew according to custom. Annually, the
two communities' total catch is estimated to be 3500 tons.

It is proposed that the present fleet should be completely replaced
by 40 motorised launches operating from a small harbour (see map,
p. 191). The craft recommended (see IFI/388B/421/76) are 'Pisces'
class 50 hp launches, which can increase the catch considerably. The
launches are available from the Yugoslav suppliers (Barkexport, Split)
at A. 50,000 each, under a special bilateral trade agreement (see
Official Gazette for 31-5-74). The new craft could exploit the local
fish resources adequately (UN/47/3001/74) and yield an annual catch
of 250 tons/boat – a total catch of 10,000 tons a year. The fish processing plant would pay A. 10/q for landed fish, the men being paid on a
regular wage basis. Ownership, and net profits, would be in the hands
of the cooperative. Each launch will have eight crew members, but
two of those must be qualified seamen (which the present fishermen
are not) and thus must either come from elsewhere on the coast or be
trained. We have, therefore, a reduction in total ' fleet ' employment
from 420 at present to 320 jobs. Clearly, it would be desirable to
start the training of suitable local fishermen in the relevant naviga-
tional, engineering and fishing skills as soon as possible.

The Technical Appendix (below) gives the details of operating
accounts for the craft and the fleet as a whole.

(3) Filleting and Freezing Plant

It is proposed to set up a small filleting and freezing plant near the
quay at Betaville. It would take in some 10,000 tons of fish a year
and produce some 6,500 tons of frozen fillets (the waste matter in a
valpy is very small) in boxes which would be collected by the National
Fish Corporation's trucks for rapid delivery to Metropole and paid for
at the standard ex-plant price adjusted for transport costs.

The plant can be supplied, net of all costs on a 'turnkey' basis by
the local construction firm of Equipo S.A. (in partnership with Team
International, U.K.) for A. 20 million (see Hadrian Report). The
total employment given would be for some eight skilled men (mechanics,
overseers etc.) and 100 women, these latter being engaged in the

simple but delicate task of filleting. So the plant is easy to operate and involves a great deal of manual labour in the processing. Similar installation has been operated successfully for some years at Omegaville, about a hundred miles up the coast. The plant could be the start for a light-industrial base in the area, and would provide work for some of the women who were previously curing fish caught under the traditional system. Electricity supplies can be obtained from the National Grid line running along the main road two miles inland, and fresh water can be pumped up from the river ,for cleansing and ice-making.

The operating account is shown in the Technical Appendix below, which shows the considerable annual gain to the cooperative and the overall profitability of this particular project, given the constraint of the ex-factory frozen fillet price offered by the National Fish Corporation. This will presumably generate greater profits to this latter enterprise, but these benefits have not been included.

(4) *Infrastructure Requirements*

In order that the project should be possible at all, substantial infrastructure works will be required. These are:

(a) a deep-water quay (20 feet deep) for the 40 launches (A. 4.0 million);

(b) improvement of the road/bridge link between Betaville and Alphaville, in order to gain access to Metropole (A. 1.2 million);

(c) construction of a community centre (including health facilities) in Betaville (A 1.0 million).

It has already been agreed that the Ministry of Public Works (see Presidential Decree No. 467 of 1976) should be responsible for infrastructure provision in Special Project Areas, of which this is one. The total capital cost of the works would be A. 5.2 million (see Technical Appendix below).

The *harbour works* (see Hadrian Report) would involve dredging the Betaville bank of the river to a depth of 20 feet, the erection of a concrete quay (some 500 feet long) for mooring purposes (the tides are not extreme in this area, the total variation being of the order of 8 feet) and the provision of fuel storage facilities, net drying sheds, simple repair facilities and so on. For painting etc. boats could be beached on the opposite bank, but major engine repairs would be carried out at the Metropole shipyard of the NFC. The *road regrading* is necessary in order to improve the road transport links to Metropole, principally to handle the NFC trucks. It is estimated that some eight trucks a day will be arriving. The present dirt road should be upgraded to tarmac, and the wooden bridge replaced by a simple steel Bailey Bridge. The *community centre* will include a clinic and training facilities as well as the space for recreation, cooperative meetings and so on. It is normal government procedure in those cases for the Ministry responsible to pay the capital costs and also to maintain the buildings, but the actual operations (staffing etc.) over and above this are to be financed by the community itself.

(5) *Cost–Benefit Analysis*

In accordance with current practice in project appraisal, a cost-benefit analysis has been carried out. No attempt has been made to use shadow prices as the Planning Commission has indicated (letter to Dr E. Knox of 26.2.76, from the permanent Secretary of the Commission) that the main focus of interest is to be the direct net benefit to the communities themselves, rather than the economy as a whole—although this of course would be considered also.

In response to initial concern expressed by some members of the Joint Committee on Special Projects, two alternative approaches to the transfer from traditional to modern fishing have been devised. Both assume that the full replacement of one by the other will take place, but one (Plan A) involves immediate elimination of traditional fishing, while the other (Plan B) allows for a gradual transfer over five years, traditional and modern forms existing side by side during that period. The results are shown below, assuming a 30-year project life and a 10 per cent discount rate.

	Net Present Value (A. m.)	
	Plan A	Plan B
Net economic benefits to community	9.54	7.35
Infrastructure cost to Government	7.65	7.55
Total	1.89	−0.20
Internal rate of return	14%	9%

As can be seen, Plan B leads to lower economic benefits to the Alpha–Beta community than Plan A, and a loss to the economy as a whole when the government expenditure on infrastructure is taken into account. The Plan B figures are lower because of the delay in reaping the full benefits of the project and the possibility of phasing infrastructure expenditure over a slightly longer period. Plan A is preferable as far as the economy as a whole is concerned, and in fact the project as a whole is only economically feasible if this alternative is chosen.

The distribution of benefits between the members of the community is shown below, in the form of annual net incomes generated by the traditional methods and by full modernisation.

ECONOMIC BENEFITS TO THE COMMUNITY (A.'000/annum)

		Traditional	Modern
Wages and salaries :	Fishing	—	1200
:	Factory	—	200
NFCU profits :	Fishing	—	200
:	Factory	—	500
Traditional craft earnings		1050	—
Total		1050	2100

The substantial increment in incomes implied by modernisation is immediately clear: in fact, total annual income to the community will be doubled. However, the employment pattern generated does differ considerably as the next table shows. Although under Plan B the employment change over would be more gradual, the consequence of operating the filleting and freezing plant below capacity would be to generate considerable losses over the transition period.

PROJECT EMPLOYMENT ESTIMATES

	Total at Present	Future: Fishing	Factory	Total
Skilled	–	80	8	88
Unskilled	420	240	100	340
Total	420	320	108	428

As a secondary effect of the project itself, the higher level of income in the community will generate higher levels of expenditure, and in consequence there will be a demand for more shops, artisan activities, new construction activities, recreation facilities and so on, as well as more direct effects such as ship servicing, net repairing and general port works. This will have a multiplier effect on employment, and based on the experience of development projects of a similar scale elsewhere in Arcadia, we would expect additional jobs to be created at a ratio of about 1.5 to every one in the project itself. This should compensate for the loss of female employment in fish curing, and probably will absorb many of those previously engaged in traditional fishing. Further, the greatly increased activity in the community will create a demand for food, and thus local agricultural products, so that there will be scope for increasing the area under cultivation and thus even more job opportunities. In our opinion, the overall result will be to attract a considerable number of people from outside the Alpha–Beta area, because the total number of jobs should reach one thousand once the project has achieved its full effect.

(6) *Conclusion*

In aggregate terms – that is for the community of Alphaville and Betaville – the project is clearly feasible in economic terms, under Plan A or Plan B, although the former would be preferable. From the point of view of the economy of Arcadia as a whole, the project would only really be justified under Plan A, as similar secondary benefits could also be obtained from public investment in development projects elsewhere. In the absence of specific instructions, and without information as to appropriate weights, we have not been able to apply any income-distribution criteria to the project.

The Project Committee might wish to apply these, taking into account the fact that average incomes in the project area are about a third of the mean for Arcadia as a whole. If this were to be done, we believe that the social benefits of the project would be much more clearly seen than in the economic analysis requested by the Client. Further on this theme it is worth noting that although the total income will be increased, it will now be spread from men toward women, fewer men will have full-time employment, and the Co-operative will have considerable economic power, controlling a substantial share of the village income. This change could have potentially disruptive consequences unless equitable mechanisms for the use of this money are developed. In particular, the cooperative might be able to finance (e.g. through wage payments) the development of other projects in the immediate vicinity, or organise service enterprises with preferential employment for unemployed fishermen.

In sum, we wholeheartedly recommend this project, which with adequate provisions for initial administration and encouragement for private enterprise to ensure efficient use of the facilities will undoubtedly contribute in a useful way to the development of Arcadia. In the wise words of *The Common People's Charter*: 'Local enterprise will provide a firm foundation for Arcadia's future.'

E. Knox
IFI Mission
Metropole

September 1976

Technical Appendix

TABLE 1

OPERATIONS ACCOUNT FOR 'PISCES' LAUNCHES

Annual Account		A./craft	Total (A.'000)
Labour[a]	skilled	12,000	480
	unskilled	18,000	720
Materials[b]		6,850	274
Amortisation[c]		8,150	326
TOTAL COSTS		45,000	1,800
Sales[d]		50,000	2,000
Profit[e]		5,000	200

[a] 2 skilled men @ A.120/week × 50 = A.12,000
   6 unskilled men @ A.60/week × 50 = A.18,000
[b] Fuel, repairs etc.
[c] 10 years @ 10 per cent; capital charge = 0.163 × A.50,000 = A.8,150
[d] A.200/ton × 250 tons = A.50,000
[e] To NFU Cooperative

TABLE 2

OPERATIONS ACCOUNT FOR FILLETING AND FREEZING PLANT

Annual Account			A.'000	
Fixed:	Administration		300	
	Maintenance		500	
	Amortisation[a]		2200	
				3000
Variable:				
	Labour:	skilled[b]	50	
		unskilled[c]	150	
	Inputs:	fish	2000	
		other[d]	800	
				3000
TOTAL COSTS				6000
Sales[e]				6500
Profit				500

[a]25 years at $10\% = 0.110 \times$ A.20m $=$ A.2.2 m

[b]8 skilled $\times$ A.125/week $\times 50 =$ A.50,000

[c]100 women $\times$ A.30/week $\times 50 =$ A.150,000

[d]Fuel, boxes etc.

[e]6,500 tons of frozen fillets output/year @ A.1000/ton; ex-factory price.

[f]To NFU cooperative.

TABLE 3

COST OF INFRASTRUCTURE PROVISION

	Initial Capital Cost (A. m)	Annual Maintenance (A. '000)	NPV over 30 years (A. m)
Harbour[a]	4.00	200	5.89
Road[b]	1.20	60	1.76
Economic infrastructure	5.20	260	7.65
Community Centre	1.00	50	1.42
Total Infrastructure	6.20	310	9.07

[a]Dredging	2.00	[b]5 miles @ A.0.2m. =	1.00
Civil works	1.50	Bridge =	0.20
Equipment	0.50		—
	4·00		1.20

Report from The Institute of Social Studies

(1) *Introduction*

Last January the Director of the Institute of Social Studies at Metropole University was invited by the Joint Committee for Special Area Planning to participate in a feasibility study for a small development project on the Arcadian Coast. It had been proposed that a joint harbour facility should be provided for two neighbouring fishing villages, Alphaville and Betaville, and that a plant for freezing fish fillets should be established. The project also provided for local road improvements, a new clinic and a community centre.

The Director of the Institute was delighted to accept this invitation, welcoming the opportunity to participate in a Government development project and noting that the President himself had stressed the need to extend the range of considerations which should be involved in the appraisal of development projects. The Institute was also pleased to cooperate with the IFI team investigating the economic aspects of the project, and found the brief collaboration instructive.

Dr. S. Robbo took charge of the project in June and, after a series of preliminary visits to the area, conducted a short survey of Alphaville and Betaville. In this he was assisted by four research students from the Institute who lived in the villages for three weeks in August.

(2) *Background to the Two Communities*

The part of the Arcadian coast where the two communities are situated is renowned for a particularly delicious fish (locally called the Valpy) which is eaten fresh locally and sun-cured for marketing inland. Shoals of valpy can be found as much as twelve miles out to sea but fishing operations are currently restricted by the range of local boats to about two miles from the shore. These boats are beached, and are therefore small, but the growing preference of the more successful fisherman for outboard motors and larger, stronger nylon nets has led to local interest in increasing the size and range of the boats. Leaders have in recent years been petitioning their Member of Parliament and the District Administration at Deltaville (38 miles away) for a new harbour which will provide for the berthing rather than beaching of boats.

The project with which this report is concerned is a response to these requests. It has been noted that local people have also been clamouring for a clinic, and it is proposed that this facility should be incorporated within the project. The needs of the two communities concerned, Alphaville and Betaville, are sufficiently similar to enable planners to design all facilities on the assumption that they will be shared. It is intended that the road through Alphaville and Betaville should be improved, and it has been noted that in a few years the effect of the project as a whole will probably have been to unite the two villages as a single, continuous settlement. With this in mind, it is proposed that a new community centre be built mid-way between Alphaville and Betaville (see map, p. 191), and the clinic located beside it.

A general feature of the scheme will be the extension of the activities of the National Fishermen's Cooperative Union in the two villages. There have been branches of the NFCU in both communities for some years, but membership and activities are very limited. The NFCU has, for example, taken very little interest in the marketing of sun-dried fish. Under the terms of the project the NFCU will participate extensively in the organisation of the fishing itself, the processing, and the marketing of the frozen fillets. Planners have stressed that the scheme is directed against local poverty. At the moment householders without boats are dependent on employment on boats operated by other householders. Households without the capital resources to participate directly in fishing will now be encouraged to take part in NFCU boat ownership schemes.

Although local history is rather vague, it seems clear that Alphaville was founded about 200 years ago by the Alpha family and that about 60 years later the Beta family moved out of the village across the river to set up a new settlement now called Betaville. The move appears to have been caused by a dispute over fishing rights. Although relationships have been strained from time to time ever since, the dispute was resolved by an agreement that fishing rights for each community should be reckoned in terms of a notional line running from the mouth of the river out to a small island about three miles from the shore, Alphaville fishing to the west, Betaville to the east (see map). Today the rights to particular fishing areas are regulated in each community by an assembly of all the boat-owning householders. This council also deals with all other affairs which do not fall within the purview of the District Council or other bodies, and is recognized by the Arcadian government as a 'village council'. Leadership of each council is supposedly elective, but has been held by the descendants of Alpha and Beta respectively for as long as anyone can remember.

The social organisation of the two villages is very similar. The settlement pattern is closely nucleated, and buildings vary from five-room brick-built houses with metal roofs to small thatched houses around the settlement perimeter. Each house is quite distinct as a social unit, the household being the principal unit of economic and political organisation within the village. Both villages are almost exclusively Roman Catholic; each has a small chapel served by a visiting priest responsible for these and two other communities. There is no local lineage organisation; kinship is reckoned bilaterally, with inheritance of gardens and 'female' property matrilateral, boats and 'male' property, including houses, patrilateral. Domestic growth may extend to three, sometimes four generations; family headship is, however, ceded to a son when the father can no longer take an active role in fishing. The villages are mainly dependent on fishing, cash income being derived almost entirely from the sale of dried fish inland. Fishing involves a pronounced division of labour; boats are owned by households, 'mastership' of a boat being a function of the household head. With the present small boats, crews of three or four are the norm; a man without sons or grandsons hires crewmen from other (often boatless) households on a share-catch basis. Women are allowed nowhere near the boats and are excluded from all fishing activities. They are, however, responsible for the drying of the fish and its marketing (by river and road) inland. Each household has its own gardens in an area around the town (see map). Beyond this there is forest, so there is no shortage of land for making new gardens, but land close to each community is at a premium. Women are wholly responsible for the gardening; rice, the main staple, is purchased from outside the area, and only fruit and vegetables are grown locally.

(3) *Sociological Problems Presented by the Project*

Set against this outline of community organisation the proposed project raises a number of sociological questions. In the following sections we consider the most salient of these in the light of the ISS survey data, and suggest ways in which our findings should be brought to bear on the evaluation of the project. Firstly we must specify the social changes which are either intended or implicit in the basic plan:

(a) Provision of a new technical base for the local economy from which a series of new activities are expected to arise, and which is expected to provide the basis for the 'modernisation' of the two villages.

(b) Modification of the economic organisation to improve opportunities for cash earning; reorganisation of fishing and processing, and changes in marketing arrangements.

(c) Extension of the activities of the main cooperative (NFCU). (Implementation of the project is dependent on an 'obligation to cooperate').

(d) To initiate a process by which the two communities will develop into a single economic, political and social unit.

The most important implicit changes are:

(e) Restructuring of the working relationships among men and among women (in boat and factory), with a consequent restructuring of the domestic relationships *between* men and women.

(f) Development of entrepreneurial activity within the fishing industry, and the provision of new economic opportunities in service and other sectors.

(g) Changes in the existing pattern of socio-economic differentiation, and in the present disposition of political authority.

In an attempt to elucidate these issues a brief survey of the two villages was carried out by the ISS team. It was decided to collect a limited amount of information from *all* economically active persons (hereafter simply described as 'adults') in the two villages, rather than attempting to conduct a more detailed sample survey. It was felt that this would provide up-to-date census material for the project, and would provide an accurate basis for the canvassing of attitudes. It should be noted that outline plans for the project had been discussed at public meetings in both villages and that the survey established, on the basis of a checklist, that virtually all adults knew something of the proposed harbour, launches, factory, road improvements, clinic and community centre. It should also be noted that the ISS survey was addressed to the general specifications of the scheme and not to the alternative modes of implementation (Plan A and Plan B), which were suggested after the survey had been carried out. Accordingly, opinions on these alternatives were not directly canvassed.

In the light of the main sociological issues raised by the project we have arranged the ISS data, for the purposes of this report, in terms of the categories listed below. The most general question to be asked is who, among these various categories, is in favour of the proposed project, and who is not. This was a direct test of attitudes involving the question: 'Do you think that, all things considered, you will be better off when the new project is established than you are now?'

SUMMARY OF QUESTIONNAIRE RESPONSES

		Number	Percentage responding Positively
(a)	Total adult population of both villages	893	68
	(Total population of both villages)	1716	
(b)	Total adult population of ALPHAVILLE	460	58
	Total adult population of BETAVILLE	433	79
	(These categories bear on the future growth of the two communities as a single unit)		
(c)	Heads of households dependent on fishing*	206	59

[*It should be noted that the heads of fishing households are all men.]

Heads of households dependent on other activities (e.g. shopkeepers)	37	61
(Total households)	243	
(This distinguishes households directly and indirectly involved in the project)		
(d) Fishing household heads owning NO boats	68	87
Fishing household heads owning one or more boats	138	56
(This broadly distinguishes households currently supplying labour and those with capital resources of their own, two categories which may see the costs and benefits of the project differently)		
(e) Adult *men* of both villages	450	61
Adult *women* of both villages	443	77
(Division of labour now and in the proposed project suggests important distinctions of attitude and interest among men and women)		
(f) Total adult population *under* 45 years old	750	72
Total adult population *over* 45 years old	143	55
(Interests and attitudes of older people, probably the leaders of the two villages, may bear significantly on the success of the scheme, but may contrast with the interests and attitudes of younger people)		

From this table we can see that within the overall majority favourably disposed to the basic project, there are considerable variations in opinion. Betaville adults are more positively disposed than Alphaville adults, women more than men, and younger people more than older people. It is also apparent that household heads who do not own boats are more optimistic about the scheme than those who do own boats. We may tentatively conclude that the project is likely to meet less opposition from the younger and poorer mass of the community than from the older men who are household heads, especially those who own boats. However, it is clearly this second category which currently wields the greatest influence in community affairs, and is likely to be a force to be reckoned with. As a general indication of opinion in the two villages the above figures are helpful, but further elucidation by direct and indirect testing was clearly required in the survey.

(4) Results of the Sociological Analysis

(a) Technical and Economic Change

The survey makes it evident that local resistance is not to the technical innovations, infrastructural facilities and planned amenities *per se*, but to the proposed terms of ownership, the organisation of labour and marketing, and the sitting of the new facilities.

Three-quarters of the adult males agreed that bigger boats were desirable, but many of them foresaw difficulties in terms of ownership and new crewing arrangements. The survey asked them to state the disadvantages of larger boats; many complained of the high capital cost which would make it difficult for an individual to acquire a controlling interest in the boat. A change in skippering and crewing arrangements would cause disputes, and competition from the bigger boats would be unfair to the smaller boat owners. Householders who owned no boats, and those with poorer craft, tended to feel that 'more people should share in the ownership of bigger boats'. However, 67 per cent of *all* heads of fishing households felt that eventually ownership of the new launches would and should pass into the control of individual households; only 28 per cent thought that they should be owned cooperatively through the NFCU. The largest proportion of adult men (61 per cent) felt that household heads should head the crew of the new boats, and only 9 per cent felt it was appropriate that they should be skippered by seamen from outside the two villages. 40 per cent would be happy to see a trained local man who was not a household head placed in charge of a boat.

In matters of ownership and operation there was a great deal of mistrust about the future role of the NFCU, particularly in Betaville where the chairman, one of the wealthiest household heads, was recently implicated in the collapse of a scheme to purchase nylon nets. Currently, only 33 per cent of the adult men in Alphaville, and 21 per cent in Betaville, are NFCU members. Younger people seemed to relish the prospect of working for wages, particularly on a share-purchasing basis; older men tended to point out that without the inducement of the present share-catch system the younger generation would show little interest in hard work. In general, it was the very poorest and the very richest household heads who were most enthusiastic about NFCU control of fishing; in the case of the former there was the hope of an immediate increase in income, and for the latter there was the attraction of being able to acquire a controlling interest in one or more boats, if not control over the whole NFCU operation.

The reorganisation of processing principally concerns the women of the two villages whom, it is hoped, will supply most of the labour for the new factory. Rumours of high wages have made a majority of women very optimistic: 64 per cent of the adult women said that they will probably seek work in the factory. Nearly all the women from boatless households (91 per cent) said that they would seek factory work. Although no questions were specifically asked about women's present role in curing and marketing fish, it was apparent that many assumed that these activities would continue alongside factory employment. A substantial 33 per cent of adult men said that they would strongly *disapprove* of a woman member of their household working in the factory, the usual reason being that this would distract them from their domestic responsibilities. Many men, however, shrugged off the question, saying that it was the business of the women to make up their own minds.

The women were generally unenthusiastic about NFCU membership and about NFCU control of fish marketing. 54 per cent of them disapproved of this monopoly, complaining that it would disrupt long-established trading arrangements, many aspects of which they valued. Questions about marketing evoked relatively little interest among the men, who tended to tell the interviewers 'you must ask my wife about that '.

In general, it seems that women are quite well disposed towards their proposed role in the project, but it is clear that their participation will bring far-reaching changes to domestic organisation. Presumably gardening will decline sharply, and some alternative arrangements will have to be made in many cases for the care of children. It is likely that factory employment will leave women with little time or inclination for continuing their present role in processing and marketing, and in any case virtually all the catch will be diverted to the factory. In sum, we would guess that the women are more likely to adjust to rapid change than the men, even if the effects of rapid change will disrupt their domestic life to a greater extent in the long run.

(b) *The Merging of Alphaville and Betaville*

The success of the proposed scheme clearly depends on close co-operation between the two villages, in the immediate future and in the long term. Given the existing rivalry between the two communities it may be foreseen that the project will inevitably be affected by factionalism in its early stages. The location of the new facilities is already a source of contention, going some way to accounting for the more positive attitude of the people of Betaville towards the basic plan. The people of Alphaville often asked interviewers why it was not possible for them to have their own harbour and factory, and complained that the proposed location of the clinic and community centre was too much in favour of Betaville. Only 61 per cent of the Alphaville adults thought that the proposed location of the harbour was a sensible choice (from a technical point of view it is the *only* choice). While 88 per cent of the Betaville people approved of the site of the clinic and community centre, only 31 per cent of the Alphaville people thought this reasonable. They often pointed out that the indirect gains to the Betaville people, particularly in land sales and opportunities to start new service businesses, would be much greater. However, it was notable that roughly half of the population of both villages (47 per cent in Alphaville, 55 per cent in Betaville) regarded the long-term development of the two villages into a single 'town' favourably. It was generally agreed that the division of fishing rights should disappear, but the chairman of the Alphaville village council pointed out that the customary legal complexities of this were such that any change would necessarily involve protracted negotiations.

It seems that this political division will affect most seriously the participation of local people in the management of the project – elections and appointments to the local NFCU branch, routine processes of decision making while the project is under way, and so on. While the safest strategy may be to exclude local people from the management of the scheme in its early stages, this carries the risk of further diminishing local enthusiasm for the project and for NFCU activities. Once the economic activities of the two villages are firmly under a single management structure it is likely that the social and political divisions between them will rapidly diminish in significance. It is possible that a more favourable attitude to the project in Alphaville could be bought by redistributing the proposed amenities more in their favour. Such an approach could be costly and technically difficult. It is tempting to argue that if the facilities are presented to the people as a *fait accompli* they will eventually accept them, but if they are invited to discuss the location of amenities this will only exacerbate the division of interest between the two villages.

(c) *The Distribution of Benefits*

A survey of the kind conducted cannot hope to throw very much light on one of the most important questions: 'who stands to gain most from the implementation of this project?' Members of the Special Projects Committee will not need to be reminded of our President's concern for the eradication of poverty and the creation of new economic opportunities. The general guidelines for this are laid down in *The Common People's Charter*, and epitomised in our Government's watchword: 'All Arcadia for All Arcadians'. In these terms, the apparent enthusiasm of the poorer people of Alphaville and Betaville for the proposed project is a good omen. Likewise, youth is apparently on the side of the project, suggesting that in due course the scheme will prosper. The National Council for Women will undoubtedly welcome the new opportunities which are being provided as enthusiastically as the women of the two villages themselves. In short, the basic project seems very much in tune with the social commitments of Arcadia.

Although it is apparent that the household heads are reluctant about giving up their control of fishing, it is evident that the younger people regard wage-earning as a release from the constraints of the present share-catch system. However, it is also clear that the leading household heads will not easily relinquish their authority, and inevitably it is with them that government personnel will have to deal, at least in the initial stages of the project. The wealthiest households are already buying up pieces of land around the river mouth and seeking licences to run garage, retailing and other businesses. The 37 non-fishing household heads are divided in their opinions about how they will fare under the scheme; some clearly look forward to expanding their retail and service businesses, but others, particularly older women traders with a very small turnover, felt that their livelihood is threatened. Few local poeple seem to think that an invasion of outsiders was likely, but when the question was put to them: 'Do you think that people from outside Alphaville and Betaville should be given jobs on the new boats and in the new factory?' only 11 per cent answered affirmatively.

(d) *The Alternative Plans*

In the light of its survey data, the ISS team feels that a gradual phasing-in of the new boats (i.e. Plan B) will be in the long term interest of the project as a whole and the people of the two villages. There seems little doubt that immediate transfer to the new scheme is the most favourable economic solution, and it could also be said that Plan A, although drastic, would have the effect of eliminating much of the incipient opposition to the project before it could become overt. However, it is doubtful that this approach would be in the long-term interest of the two villages, and might well diminish local enthusiasm for the project. Plan A would demand the application of considerable external authority, if not force, while Plan B would presumably allow for the changes to be negotiated with the people themselves. The fact that the people are, on the whole, favourably disposed to the basic plan does not seem to warrant immediate and draconian realisation of that plan. It seems that many boat-owners imagine that they will be able to use the existing small craft alongside the new launches, and point out that the small boats have functions (river communications, shell fish collection) which bigger boats could not perform. The existing boats are usually objects of family pride, and there may be strong sentimental obstacles to replacing them. If they are not eliminated, it is doubtful whether legal sanctions or such measures as removing net-stanchions will meet with much success.

A five-year phasing-in of the project should allow sufficient time for the people and the project administrators to come to terms with the following outstanding problems:

(i)   The transference of control over fishing, processing and marketing to the NFCU; it seems that the present NFCU organisation in both villages, firmly in the grip of local patrons, is an insecure basis for the greatly extended role envisaged for the cooperative.

(ii)   The reconciliation of differences between Alphaville and Betaville; an optimum solution may be to rearrange and reconstitute the village councils so that they become, *de facto*, a single NFCU branch.

(iii)   The adjustment of both men and women to new working arrangements; sudden disruption of the family economy could have deleterious effects on the project as a whole.

(iv)   The equitable distribution of gains throughout the community; a rapid change-over may enable a few people to get quick access to power and wealth, at the expense of others.

However, the fact that a more gradual implementation of the project will reduce the economic returns to the people is in itself an argument

in favour of Plan A. It could be said that the enthusiasm of the local
people is ultimately dependent on the size of the material rewards
offered, and how soon these rewards appear. There is a sense in
which the compliance of most individuals can be bought for a price.
The major question here is whether, in the long run, the cost to the
community of Plan A is likely to be great enough to justify a preference
for Plan B.

November 1976   Dr S. Robbo
                                       Institute of Social Studies
                                       University of Metropole
                                       Arcadia

PRESENT VALUE OF £1 AT RATE r PAYABLE IN t YEARS: $(1+r)^{-t}$

t	2%	3%	4%	5%	6%	7%	8%	9%	10%	11%	12%	13%	14%	15%	16%	18%	20%	25%
1	0.980	0.971	0.962	0.952	0.943	0.935	0.926	0.917	0.909	0.901	0.893	0.885	0.877	0.870	0.862	0.847	0.833	0.800
2	0.961	0.943	0.925	0.907	0.890	0.873	0.857	0.842	0.826	0.812	0.797	0.783	0.769	0.756	0.743	0.718	0.694	0.640
3	0.942	0.915	0.889	0.864	0.840	0.816	0.794	0.772	0.751	0.731	0.712	0.693	0.675	0.658	0.641	0.609	0.579	0.512
4	0.924	0.888	0.855	0.823	0.792	0.763	0.735	0.708	0.683	0.659	0.636	0.613	0.592	0.572	0.552	0.516	0.482	0.410
5	0.906	0.863	0.822	0.784	0.747	0.713	0.681	0.650	0.621	0.593	0.567	0.543	0.519	0.497	0.476	0.437	0.402	0.328
6	0.888	0.837	0.790	0.746	0.705	0.666	0.630	0.596	0.564	0.535	0.507	0.480	0.456	0.432	0.410	0.370	0.335	0.262
7	0.871	0.813	0.760	0.711	0.665	0.623	0.583	0.547	0.513	0.482	0.452	0.425	0.400	0.376	0.354	0.314	0.279	0.210
8	0.853	0.789	0.731	0.677	0.627	0.582	0.540	0.502	0.467	0.434	0.404	0.376	0.351	0.327	0.305	0.266	0.233	0.168
9	0.837	0.766	0.703	0.645	0.592	0.544	0.500	0.460	0.424	0.391	0.361	0.333	0.308	0.284	0.263	0.225	0.194	0.134
10	0.820	0.744	0.676	0.614	0.558	0.508	0.463	0.422	0.386	0.352	0.322	0.295	0.270	0.247	0.227	0.191	0.162	0.107
11	0.804	0.722	0.650	0.585	0.527	0.475	0.429	0.388	0.350	0.317	0.287	0.261	0.237	0.215	0.195	0.162	0.135	0.086
12	0.788	0.701	0.625	0.557	0.497	0.444	0.397	0.356	0.319	0.286	0.257	0.231	0.208	0.187	0.168	0.137	0.112	0.069
13	0.773	0.681	0.601	0.530	0.469	0.415	0.368	0.326	0.290	0.258	0.229	0.204	0.182	0.163	0.145	0.116	0.093	0.055
14	0.758	0.661	0.577	0.505	0.442	0.388	0.340	0.299	0.263	0.232	0.205	0.181	0.160	0.141	0.125	0.099	0.078	0.044
15	0.743	0.642	0.555	0.481	0.417	0.362	0.315	0.275	0.239	0.209	0.183	0.160	0.140	0.123	0.108	0.084	0.065	0.035
16	0.728	0.623	0.534	0.458	0.394	0.339	0.292	0.252	0.218	0.188	0.163	0.141	0.123	0.107	0.093	0.071	0.054	0.028
17	0.714	0.605	0.513	0.436	0.371	0.317	0.270	0.231	0.198	0.170	0.146	0.125	0.108	0.093	0.080	0.060	0.045	0.023
18	0.700	0.587	0.494	0.416	0.350	0.296	0.250	0.212	0.180	0.153	0.130	0.111	0.095	0.081	0.069	0.051	0.038	0.018
19	0.686	0.570	0.475	0.396	0.331	0.277	0.232	0.194	0.164	0.138	0.116	0.098	0.083	0.070	0.060	0.043	0.031	0.014
20	0.673	0.554	0.456	0.377	0.312	0.258	0.215	0.178	0.149	0.124	0.104	0.087	0.073	0.061	0.051	0.037	0.026	0.012
21	0.660	0.538	0.439	0.359	0.294	0.242	0.199	0.164	0.135	0.112	0.093	0.077	0.064	0.053	0.044	0.031	0.022	0.009
22	0.647	0.522	0.422	0.342	0.278	0.226	0.184	0.150	0.123	0.101	0.083	0.068	0.056	0.046	0.038	0.026	0.018	0.007
23	0.634	0.507	0.406	0.326	0.262	0.211	0.170	0.138	0.112	0.091	0.074	0.060	0.049	0.040	0.033	0.022	0.015	0.006
24	0.622	0.492	0.390	0.310	0.247	0.197	0.158	0.126	0.102	0.082	0.066	0.053	0.043	0.035	0.028	0.019	0.013	0.005
25	0.610	0.478	0.375	0.295	0.233	0.184	0.146	0.116	0.092	0.074	0.059	0.047	0.038	0.030	0.024	0.016	0.010	0.004
26	0.598	0.464	0.361	0.281	0.220	0.172	0.135	0.106	0.084	0.066	0.053	0.042	0.033	0.026	0.021	0.014	0.009	0.003
27	0.586	0.450	0.347	0.268	0.207	0.161	0.125	0.098	0.076	0.060	0.047	0.037	0.029	0.023	0.018	0.011	0.007	0.002
28	0.574	0.437	0.333	0.255	0.196	0.150	0.116	0.090	0.069	0.054	0.042	0.033	0.026	0.020	0.016	0.010	0.006	0.002
29	0.563	0.424	0.321	0.243	0.185	0.141	0.107	0.082	0.063	0.048	0.037	0.029	0.022	0.017	0.014	0.008	0.005	0.002
30	0.552	0.412	0.308	0.231	0.174	0.131	0.099	0.075	0.057	0.044	0.033	0.026	0.020	0.015	0.012	0.007	0.004	0.001
40	0.453	0.307	0.208	0.142	0.097	0.067	0.046	0.032	0.022	0.015	0.011	0.008	0.005	0.004	0.003	0.001	0.001	
50	0.372	0.228	0.141	0.087	0.054	0.034	0.021	0.013	0.009	0.005	0.003	0.002	0.001	0.001	0.001			

TABLE 2

Present Value at Rate r of the Sum of N Annual Instalments of £1 Payable at End of Year:

$$\sum_{t=1}^{N} \frac{1}{(1+r)^t} = \frac{1}{r}\left\{1 - \frac{1}{(1+r)^N}\right\}$$

N \ r	2%	3%	4%	5%	6%	7%	8%	9%	10%	11%	12%	13%	14%	15%	16%	18%	20%	25%
1	0.980	0.971	0.962	0.952	0.943	0.935	0.926	0.917	0.909	0.901	0.893	0.885	0.877	0.870	0.862	0.847	0.833	0.800
2	1.942	1.913	1.886	1.859	1.833	1.808	1.783	1.759	1.736	1.713	1.690	1.668	1.647	1.626	1.605	1.566	1.528	1.440
3	2.884	2.829	2.775	2.723	2.673	2.624	2.577	2.531	2.487	2.444	2.402	2.361	2.322	2.283	2.246	2.174	2.106	1.952
4	3.808	3.717	3.630	3.546	3.465	3.387	3.312	3.240	3.170	3.102	3.037	2.974	2.914	2.855	2.798	2.690	2.589	2.362
5	4.713	4.580	4.452	4.329	4.212	4.100	3.993	3.890	3.791	3.696	3.605	3.517	3.433	3.352	3.274	3.127	2.991	2.689
6	5.601	5.417	5.242	5.076	4.917	4.767	4.623	4.486	4.355	4.231	4.111	3.998	3.889	3.784	3.685	3.498	3.326	2.951
7	6.472	6.230	6.002	5.786	5.582	5.389	5.206	5.033	4.868	4.712	4.564	4.423	4.288	4.160	4.039	3.812	3.605	3.161
8	7.325	7.020	6.733	6.463	6.210	5.971	5.747	5.535	5.335	5.146	4.968	4.799	4.639	4.487	4.344	4.078	3.837	3.329
9	8.162	7.786	7.435	7.108	6.802	6.515	6.247	5.995	5.759	5.537	5.328	5.132	4.946	4.772	4.607	4.303	4.031	3.463
10	8.983	8.530	8.111	7.722	7.360	7.024	6.710	6.418	6.145	5.889	5.650	5.426	5.216	5.019	4.833	4.494	4.192	3.571
11	9.787	9.253	8.760	8.306	7.887	7.499	7.139	6.805	6.495	6.207	5.988	5.687	5.453	5.234	5.029	4.656	4.327	3.656
12	10.575	9.954	9.385	8.863	8.384	7.943	7.536	7.161	6.814	6.492	6.194	5.918	5.660	5.421	5.197	4.793	4.439	3.725
13	11.343	10.635	9.986	9.394	8.853	8.358	7.904	7.487	7.103	6.750	6.424	6.122	5.842	5.583	5.342	4.910	4.533	3.780
14	12.106	11.296	10.563	9.899	9.295	8.745	8.244	7.786	7.367	6.982	6.628	6.302	6.002	5.724	5.468	5.008	4.611	3.824
15	12.849	11.938	11.118	10.380	9.712	9.108	8.559	8.061	7.606	7.191	6.811	6.462	6.142	5.847	5.575	5.092	4.675	3.859
16	13.578	12.561	11.652	10.838	10.106	9.447	8.851	8.313	7.824	7.379	6.974	6.604	6.265	5.954	5.669	5.162	4.730	3.887
17	14.292	13.166	12.166	11.274	10.477	9.763	9.122	8.544	8.022	7.549	7.120	6.729	6.373	6.047	5.749	5.222	4.775	3.910
18	14.992	13.753	12.659	11.690	10.828	10.059	9.372	8.756	8.201	7.702	7.250	6.840	6.467	6.128	5.818	5.273	4.812	3.928
19	15.678	14.324	13.134	12.085	11.158	10.336	9.604	8.950	8.365	7.839	7.366	6.938	6.550	6.198	5.877	5.316	4.844	3.942
20	16.351	14.877	13.590	12.462	11.470	10.594	9.818	9.129	8.514	7.963	7.469	7.025	6.623	6.259	5.929	5.353	4.870	3.954
21	17.011	15.415	14.029	12.821	11.764	10.836	10.017	9.292	8.649	8.075	7.562	7.102	6.687	6.312	5.973	5.384	4.891	3.963
22	17.658	15.937	14.451	13.163	12.042	11.061	10.201	9.442	8.772	8.176	7.645	7.170	6.743	6.359	6.011	5.410	4.909	3.970
23	18.292	16.444	14.857	13.489	12.303	11.272	10.371	9.580	8.883	8.266	7.718	7.230	6.792	6.399	6.044	5.432	4.925	3.976
24	18.914	16.936	15.247	13.799	12.550	11.469	10.529	9.707	8.985	8.348	7.784	7.283	6.835	6.434	6.073	5.451	4.937	3.981
25	19.523	17.413	15.622	14.094	12.783	11.654	10.675	9.823	9.077	8.422	7.843	7.330	6.873	6.464	6.097	5.467	4.948	3.985
26	20.122	17.877	15.983	14.375	13.003	11.826	10.810	9.929	9.161	8.488	7.896	7.372	6.906	6.491	6.118	5.480	4.956	3.988
27	20.707	18.327	16.330	14.643	13.211	11.987	10.935	10.027	9.237	8.548	7.943	7.409	6.935	6.514	6.136	5.492	4.964	3.990
28	21.281	18.764	16.663	14.898	13.406	12.137	11.051	10.116	9.307	8.602	7.984	7.441	6.961	6.534	6.152	5.502	4.970	3.992
29	21.844	19.188	16.984	15.141	13.591	12.278	11.158	10.198	9.370	8.650	8.022	7.470	6.983	6.551	6.166	5.510	4.975	3.994
30	22.396	19.600	17.292	15.372	13.765	12.409	11.258	10.274	9.427	8.694	8.055	7.496	7.003	6.566	6.177	5.517	4.979	3.995
40	27.355	23.115	19.793	17.159	15.046	13.332	11.925	10.757	9.779	8.951	8.244	7.634	7.105	6.642	6.234	5.548	4.997	3.999
50	31.424	25.730	21.482	18.256	15.762	13.801	12.234	10.962	9.915	9.042	8.304	7.675	7.133	6.661	6.246	5.554	4.999	4.000

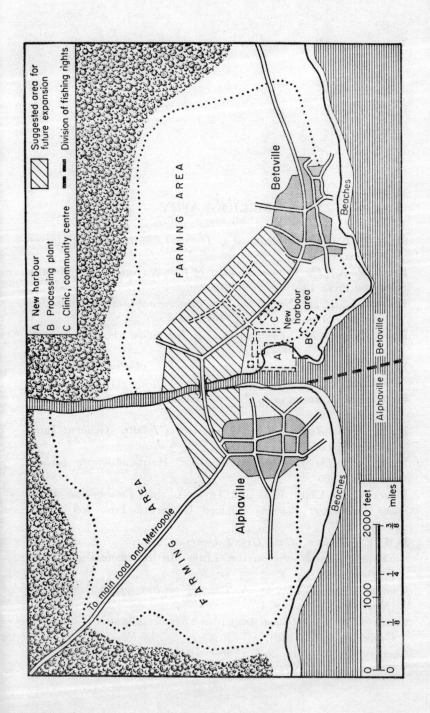

BIBLIOGRAPHY

Adler, H. A., *Economic Appraisal of Transport Projects* (Indiana University Press, 1971).

Baran, P. A., *The Political Economy of Growth* (New York: Monthly Review Press, 1957).

Barnard, C. S., and Nix, J. S., *Farm Planning and Control* (Cambridge: Cambridge University Press, 1973).

Barrett-Brown, M., *The Economics of Imperialism* (Harmondsworth, Middx: Penguin, 1974).

Baumol, W., *Economic Theory and Operations Analysis* (New York: McGraw-Hill, 1965).

Bettelheim, C., *Studies in the Theory of Planning* (London: Asia Publishing House, 1958).

Bhalla, A. S., *Technology and Development in Industry* (Geneva: International Labour Office, 1975).

Blaug, M., *The Economics of Education* (Harmondsworth, Middx: Penguin, 1968).

Blitzer, C. R., Clark, P. B. and Taylor L. (eds) *Economy-wide Models and Development Planning* (Oxford University Press for IBRD, 1975).

BOUIES, *Bulletin of the Oxford University Institute of Economics and Statistics* (special issue on the 'Little–Mirrlees manual'), (Oxford, February 1972).

Caiden, N., and Wildavsky, A., *Planning and Budgeting in Poor Countries* (New York: Wiley, 1974).

Cameron, B., *Input–Output Analysis and Resource Allocation* (Cambridge University Press, 1968).

Chenery, H. B., *et al.*, *Redistribution with Growth* (Oxford University Press for IBRD, 1974).

Dasgupta, A. K., and Pearce, D. W., *Cost-Benefit Analysis: Theory and Practice* (London: Macmillan, 1972).

Dobb, M., *An Essay on Economic Growth and Planning* (New York: Monthly Review Press, 1960).

—, *WelfareEconomics and the Economics of Socialism* (Cambridge University Press, 1970).

Dorfman, R. (ed.), *Measuring the Benefits of Government Investments* (Washington: Brookings, 1965).

—, Samuelson, P., and Solow, R., *Linear Programming and Economic Analysis* (New York: McGraw-Hill, 1958).

Eckaus, R. S., and Rosenstein-Rodan, P. N., *Analysis of Development Problems: Studies of the Chilean Economy* (Amsterdam: North-Holland, 1973).

Ellman, M., *Soviet Planning Today* (Cambridge University Press, 1971).

FitzGerald, E. V. K., *The State and Economic Development: Peru since 1968* (Cambridge University Press, 1976*a*).

—, 'Aspects of the Political Economy of the Latin-American State', *Development and Change*, 7.2 (1976*b*).

—, 'The Urban Service Sector, the Supply of Wagegoods and the Shadow Wagerate', *Oxford Economic Papers*, 28.2 (1976*c*).

—, 'The Public Investment Criterion and the Role of the State', *Journal of Development Studies*, 13.3 (1977).

Furtado, C., *Economic Development in Latin America* (Cambridge University Press, 1970).

Galenson, W., and Leibenstein, H., 'Investment Criteria, Productivity and Economic Development', *Quarterly Economic Journal* (August 1955).

Goreux, L., and Manne, A., *Multi-level Planning: Case Studies in Mexico* (Amsterdam: North-Holland, 1973).

Griffin, K., and Enos, J., *Planning Development* (London: Addison-Wesley, 1971).

Hanson, A. H., *Public Enterprise and Economic Development* (London: Routledge & Kegan Paul, 1965).

Harberger, A. C., *Project Evaluation* (London: Macmillan, 1972).

Harcourt, G. C., and Laing, N. F., *Capital and Growth* (Harmondsworth, Middx: Penguin, 1971).

Healy, J. M., *The Economics of Aid* (London: Routledge & Kegan Paul, 1971).

Hirschleifer, J., 'On the Theory of Optimal Investment Decisions', *Journal of Political Economy* (August 1958).

Hirschman, A. O., *The Strategy of Economic Development* (New Haven, Conn.: Yale University Press, 1958).

—, *Development Projects Observed* (Washington: Brookings, 1967).

IBRD, (International Bank for Reconstruction and Development), (Squire, L., and Van Der Tak, H. Q.) *Economic Analysis of Projects* (Baltimore: Johns Hopkins, 1975).

Isard, W., *Methods of Regional Analysis* (Cambridge, Mass.: M.I.T. Press, 1960).

Johnson, H. G., *Technology and Economic Interdependence* (London: Macmillan, 1975).

Judge, G. G., and Takayama, T., *Studies in Economic Planning over Space and Time* (Amsterdam: North-Holland, 1973).

Kindelberger, C. P., *Economic Development*, 2nd ed. (New York: McGraw-Hill, 1965).

King, J. A., *Economic Development Projects and Their Appraisal* (Baltimore: Johns Hopkins, 1967).

Kornai, J., *Mathematical Planning of Structural Decisions* (Amsterdam: North-Holland, 1975).

Krutilla, J. V., and Eckstein, O., *Multiple Purpose River Development* (Baltimore: Johns Hopkins, 1958).

Lal, D., *Wells and Welfare* (Paris: OECD, 1972).

—, *Appraising Foreign Investment in Developing Countries* (London: Heinemann, 1975).

Lerner, A. P., *The Economics of Control*, (New York: Macmillan, 1944).

Lewis, W. A., 'Economic Development with Unlimited Supplies of Labour', *Manchester School* (May 1954).

—, *Development Planning* (London: Allen & Unwin, 1966).

Leys, C., *Underdevelopment in Kenya* (London: Heinemann, 1975).

Lichfield, N., *Evaluating the Planning Process* (Oxford: Pergamon Press, 1976).

Little, I. M. D., *A Critique of Welfare Economics* (Oxford University Press, 1957).

Little, I. M. D., and Mirrlees, J. A., *Project Appraisal and Planning for Developing Countries* (London: Heinemann 1974).

Little, I. M. D., and Scott, M. FG., *Using Shadow Prices* (London: Heinemann, 1976).

Manne, A. S., *Investment for Capacity Expansion* (London: Allen & Unwin, 1967).

Marglin, J. A., *Approaches to Dynamic Investment Planning* (Amsterdam: North-Holland, 1963).

Marglin, J. A., *Public Investment Criteria* (London: Allen & Unwin 1967).

McKean, R., *Efficiency in Government through Systems Analysis* (New York: Wiley, 1958).

Merret, A. J., and Sykes, A., *The Finance and Analysis of Capital Projects* (London: Longmans, 1963).

Millward, R., *Public Expenditure Economics* (London: McGraw-Hill, 1971).

Mishra, S. N., and Beyer, J., *Cost–Benefit Analysis: A Case Study of the Ratnagiri Fisheries Project* (Delhi: Hindustani Publishing Corp., for the Institute of Economic Growth, 1976).

ODM. (Ministry of Overseas Development), *A Guide to Project Appraisal in Developing Countries* (London: HMSO, 1972).

OECD. (Organisation for Economic Cooperation and Development), *Manual of Industrial Project Analysis* (2 vols. and appendix), (Paris 1968).

Payer, C., *The Debt Trap* (Harmondsworth, Middx: Penguin, 1974).

Pearson, L., *Partners in Development* (Report of the Commission on International Development), (New York: Praeger 1969).

Poliquen, L., *Risk Analysis in Project Appraisal* (Washington: IBRD, 1970).

Prest, A. R., and Turvey, R., 'Cost Benefit Analysis: A Survey', *Economic Journal*, 75 (1965), 683–735.

Price-Gittinger, J., *Economic Analysis of Agricultural Projects* (Washington: IBRD 1972).

Qayum, A., *Theory and Policy of Accounting Prices* (Amsterdam: North-Holland 1963).

Radice, H., *International Firms and Modern Imperialism* (Harmondsworth, Middx: Penguin, 1975).

Radowski, M., *Efficiency of Investment in a Socialist Economy* (Oxford: Pergamon, 1966).

Reutlinger, S., *Techniques for Project Appraisal under Uncertainty* (Washington: IBRD 1970).

Roemer, M., and Stern, J. J., *The Appraisal of Development Projects* (New York: Praeger, 1975).

Sachs, I., *Patterns of Public Sector in Underdeveloped Economies* (London: Asia Publishing House, 1964).

Schumacher, E. F., *Small is Beautiful* (London: Blond & Briggs, 1973).

Scott, A. J., *Combinatorial Programming, Spatial Analysis and Planning* (London: Methuen, 1971).

Scott, M. FG., 'How to Use and Estimate Shadow Exchange Rates', *Oxford Economic Papers*, 26.2 (1974).

Scott, M. FG., MacArthur, J. D., and Newbery D. M. G., *Project Appraisal in Practice* (London: Heinemann, 1975).

Sen, A. K., *The Choice of Technique*, 3rd ed. (Oxford: Blackwell, 1968).

Sengupta, J. K., and Fox, K. A., *Optimisation Techniques in Quantitative Economic Models* (Amsterdam: North-Holland, 1971).

Seton, F., *Shadow Wages in the Chilean Economy* (Paris: OECD, 1972).

Solow, R. M., *Capital Theory and the Rate of Return* (Amsterdam: North-Holland, 1963).

Soza, H., *Planificacion del Desarrollo Industrial* (4th ed., Mexico: Siglo XXI, 1974).

Stewart, F., 'A Note on Social Cost–Benefit Analysis and Class Conflict in LDC's', *World Development*, 3.1 (1975).

Sutcliffe, R., *Industry and Underdevelopment*, (London: Addison-Wesley, 1971).

Theil, H., *Applied Economic Forecasting* (Amsterdam: North-Holland, 1971).

Tinbergen, J., *Development Planning* (London: Weidenfeld & Nicolson, 1967).

Todaro, M. P., 'A Model of Labour Migration and Urban Unemployment in Less-Developed Countries ', *American Economic Review*, LIX. 1 (1969).

—, *Development Planning* (Nairobi: Oxford University Press, 1971).

Turner, J., *Forecasting Practices in British Industry* (Guildford: Surrey University Press, 1974).

UN (United Nations), *Manual on Economic Development Projects* (New York, 1958).

UNIDO (United Nations Industrial Development Organisation), *Guidelines for Project Evaluation* (New York, 1972).

Vaitsos, C., *Intercountry Income Distribution and Transnational Enterprises* (Oxford University Press, 1974).

Van der Tak, H. Q., *The Economic Choice between Hydroelectric and Thermal Power Developments* (Washington: IBRD, 1967).

Vaneck, J., *The General Theory of Labor-managed Market Economies* (Ithaca, N.Y.: Cornell University Press, 1970).

Waterston, A., *Development Planning: The Lessons of Experience* (Baltimore: Johns Hopkins, 1965).

White, D. J., *Dynamic Programming* (London: Oliver & Boyd, 1969).

Wolfe, H. D., *Business Forecasting Methods* (New York: Holt, 1966).

Yeomans, K. A., *Statistics for the Social Scientist*, vols 1 and 2 (Harmondsworth, Middx: Penguin, 1968).

INDEX

accounting prices, *see* shadow prices

Adler, H. A.   5, 34

aid, *see* external finance

agriculture, agricultural projects, textbooks on   5, 139; choice of cropping pattern in   91–2; use of linear programming in   131–4; mechanisation of   157–8; aid agreements for   163; *see also* irrigation

Alpha-Beta Fisheries Project xii n., 165–88

Arcadia, presidency of   165; future of 175; *Common People's Charter* of   175, 186

Bangladesh xv

Baran, P. A.   110, 150

Barnard, C. S.   139

Barrett-Brown, M.   150

Baumol, W.   134, 139

Bettelheim, C.   122

Beyer, J.   82, 165

Bhalla, A. S.   151

Blaug, M.   58

Blitzer, C. R.   139

Brazil xv

Caiden, N.   110

Cameron, B.   122

cash flow   6–9; principle of   6; estimation of   7–8; examples of   7, 11, 71, 83–4, 85, 88

Chenery, H. B.   69, 150

choice of technique   142–5; in construction   92–3; in electric power generation   156–7; in industry 151, 159–60;

in roadbuilding   162; and public works   163

commodities, valuation of   35–44; treatment of state income in   36–7; road transport costs   37, 42; textiles   39; textbooks on   43–4; examples of 72–3, 91; *see also* traded goods, non-traded goods

commodity balance,   *see*   materials balance

cost-benefit analysis, definition of xi–xii; brief history of   1–3; place in project appraisal   4; textbooks on   5; example of   71–4; in advanced economies   78–82; in Alpha-Beta Fisheries Project 172–3; *see also* externalities

cost-benefit ratio 108–10

Dasgupta, A. K.   82

Digby, M.   164

discounting, discount factor, discount rate: definition of   9–13; examples of 83–4, 85, 88, 90, 164; setting of 104–7; tables for   189–90

Dobb, M.   69

Dorfman, R.   69, 120

Dupuit, J.   2

Eckaus, R. S.   122

Eckstein, O.   34, 69

electrification   21, 23, 25–6, 156–7, 171

Ellman, M.   82, 151

Enos, J.   122

external finance   145–7; and income distribution   61–4; grant element in

197